Come to the Father

Drawing near to God
through Prayer and Scripture

Tracy Hill

© 2023 Tracy Hill

All rights reserved. Except as provided by the Copyright Act no part of this publication may be reproduced, stored in a retrieval system, or transmitted in any form or by any means without the prior written permission of the publisher.

Cover photographs copyright © Tracy Hill 2021. All rights reserved.

All Scripture quotations, unless otherwise indicated, are taken from the Holy Bible, New International Version®, NIV®. Copyright ©1973, 1978, 1984, 2011 by Biblica, Inc.™ Used by permission of Zondervan. All rights reserved worldwide. www.zondervan.com, The "NIV" and "New International Version" are trademarks registered in the United States Patent and Trademark Office by Biblica, Inc.™

NKJV: Scripture taken from the New King James Version®. Copyright © 1982 by Thomas Nelson. Used by permission. All rights reserved.

NLT: Scripture quotations marked (NLT) are taken from the *Holy Bible*, New Living Translation, copyright © 1996, 2004, 2015 by Tyndale House Foundation. Used by permission of Tyndale House Publishers, Carol Stream, Illinois 60188, USA. All rights reserved.

ISBN: 978-0-9976913-8-2

Dedicated to...

My beloved grandparents, who paved the way for my faith.

You led by example.

And I know you were praying for me all along.

Contents

A Gracious Endorsement 6

Cover Photo 7

Introduction 9

Week One	Pray This Way	 13
Week Two	Worship	 33
Week Three	Submission	 49
Week Four	Thanksgiving	 65
Week Five	Requests	 81
Week Six	Confession	 97
Week Seven	Protection	 113
Week Eight	Prayer Prompts	 129
Week Nine	Prayer Devotions	 140

Closing Encouragement *156*

Leader Guide *158*

So Grateful *162*

Getting to Know the Author *163*

More Resources *164*

A Gracious Endorsement

Prayer is the way we talk to our gracious God. It is the key to coming close to Jesus. Tracy Hill illuminates this precious spiritual discipline in her latest Bible Study, "Come to the Father: Drawing Near to God Through Prayer and Scripture." Tracy's love of Jesus shines through this miraculous nine-week journey that puts each of us face to face with our Lord. Through beautiful, heartfelt writing, Tracy gets at the core of prayer—coming to God in humility and love, with the heart of a child. She encourages us to deeply reflect on the practice of prayer, in all its magnificent forms, and to be comfortable with expressing our devotion to our loving Father through Christ. With many examples of prayer, including prompts and devotions, we are able to feel comfortable coming to Jesus with thanksgiving, requests, and confession. Tracy is a master storyteller, weaving Bible passages with her deep understanding of prayer. This is a study you will remember forever because it is life changing and affirming. We are blessed to have such a God-breathed and inspired author like Tracy to guide us on the path to deeper devotion. "Come to the Father" is very special and I urge you to be transformed by its message.

—Donna Rose Houchen
Writer, Mental Health America

Cover Photo

The well-loved, well-worn Bibles on the cover of this workbook belonged to my faith-filled grandparents—Grandma and Grandpa Leavitt, and Grandma Mary. They have lovingly been passed down to me. I am now the honored keeper of the Bibles that my loved ones held in their hands and poured over earnestly. They knew that spending time in the Word was a way of hearing from the Lord. Over the years my grandparents did more than read their Bibles, they took the messages to heart and lived them out to their fullest capacity. As a child growing up, I witnessed how their walk matched their talk. They said they loved Jesus and their words and actions revealed that they most definitely did—there was no contradiction. They consistently lived out their faith and loved others so generously. My Grandma Mary's warm, kind, and gentle spirit showed me the sincere love of Jesus. My Grandpa Leavitt has been a solid, godly patriarch for our family. My grandparents showed me the way to my Savior. They were the ones who taught me to pray. Whenever my cousins and I spent the night at Grandpa and Grandma Leavitt's house or went on a trip to their cabin in the mountains, they always said grace at mealtimes, and tucked us into bed with our prayers at night. My Grandma Leavitt is the one who prayed with me to accept Jesus into my heart—the most important prayer I've ever prayed.

"If you declare with your mouth, 'Jesus is Lord,' and believe in your heart that God raised him from the dead, you will be saved." Romans 10:9

Come to the Father

with the

Heart of a Child

Introduction

Our Heavenly Father created us to have an ever-lasting, ever-growing personal relationship with Him. From before we even took our first breath, that was His beautiful plan. He invites us to enter sweet and holy fellowship with Him and He has given us the means for communication. There is nothing more precious than a child of God and our Heavenly Father spending time together—it is a glimpse of heaven and earth brilliantly colliding.

Unfortunately, we far too often feel incompetent when it comes to prayer. We have a misconstrued notion of how prayer is supposed to look, and we feel that we fall short. We put undue pressure on ourselves to have the perfect words, to sound eloquent and religious. In reality, the Lord loves us and just wants us to share our hearts with Him, as we would with any other close relationship. Prayer is never intended to make us feel guilty.

Over the course of the next nine weeks, with *The Lord's Prayer* as our basis, we will read God's Word and use it to guide us in prayer. Scripture tells us to *"pray continually,"* and with good reason **(1 Thessalonians 5:17)**. It's our way of communicating with our Heavenly Father. My hope is that by practicing prayer daily, we will grow more confident and comfortable in talking to God on a consistent basis.

By regularly combining God's Word along with our prayers, we are brought back to the original purpose of on-going fellowship with our Heavenly Father. Whenever we open God's Word and read a sentence, a passage, or an entire book of the Bible, we have a chance to hear from the Lord directly. When we come to Him in prayer, we embrace the opportunity to share our heart, our cares and concerns with Him, and to declare His praise and worship. Through time spent in our Bibles and time devoted to prayer, we experience the blessing of God's Presence with us—we're reminded that we are not alone.

Prayer and Scripture—the two essential keys to a fulfilling personal relationship with our Father. They have the miraculous power to impact our lives beyond anything we could ask or imagine. We're reminded of God's authority and power; our eyes are opened to God's perspective; our minds are refocused on His Truth, and our hearts are aligned to His heart. Both Scripture and prayer remind us we are loved, they wash us in peace, fill us with joy, guide us toward holiness, and remind us that we have been given every spiritual blessing. We find strength, hope, and the ability to persevere. We gain wisdom and direction.

With all these blessings found in our Bibles and available to us through prayer, why would we neglect to whole-heartedly seize such an amazing opportunity to spend time with the Lord?

"My heart says of you, "Seek his face!" Your face, LORD, I will seek." Psalm 27:8

We will lay a firm foundation of who God is and we'll be reminded of who He says we are. We will discover His promises for us and begin to confidently claim them in prayer. When we base our prayers on the Word of God, they cannot help but be filled with power and truth! We will come to understand and apply what it means to *pray in Jesus' Name* and *in accord with God's will*.

I sincerely pray that the Scriptures come alive, and the Father reveals His heart to you. I also pray that you share your heart with Him, and as a result you experience His tender care. My genuine desire is that this prayer journal/Bible study/devotional (it's a little combo of all three) encourages you to draw near to God and helps you realize He has always been close to you.

"I keep asking that the God of our Lord Jesus Christ, the glorious Father, may give you the Spirit of wisdom and revelation, so that you may know him better. [18] I pray that the eyes of your heart may be enlightened in order that you may know the hope to which he has called you, the riches of his glorious inheritance in his holy people, [19] and his incomparably great power for us who believe. That power is the same as the mighty strength." Ephesians 1:17-19

The Word of God and prayer go hand-in-hand. They are equally vital in growing our faith and relationship with the Lord. In the following pages, we will apply Scripture to various aspects of prayer—topics such as praise and thanksgiving, confession, and laying our daily needs before the Lord.

In our first week, we will look at what Jesus teaches us about prayer and gain inspiration from His example. The weeks that follow will build upon His concepts with prayer applications.

"God is spirit, and his worshipers must worship in the spirit and in truth." John 4:24

God invites us to spend time with Him and asks us to make Him our number one priority! So, let's begin by purposefully taking a break from the busyness and mindfully stepping into His restful, reassuring, sovereign Presence.

Remember: In prayer there is no need for pretense; the Lord desires our authenticity. He simply wants our heart. We don't need to be perfect, just honest and sincere. Hopefully with practice, prayer will become as natural as breathing.

- Before we begin, take a moment to reflect on your prayer life currently. How would you describe it? In what ways would you like it to improve?

- Pause now and ask the Lord to help you on this prayer journey. You can write your prayer here if you like. It can be a testimony to reflect on.

The initial seven weeks will guide us through the practices of *prayer* and *Bible study*. **The eighth week** uses simple *prayer prompts* to encourage you to write your own praises and supplications to the Father. **The ninth week** provides additional *prayer devotions* to further bless and inspire our walk with the Lord. Enjoy weekly messages to go along with each lesson at "Be Blessed and Inspired with Tracy Hill" on: (more QR codes on page 164)

YouTube:    Spotify:

"Let us draw near to God with a sincere heart

and with the full assurance that faith brings..."

Hebrews 10:22

WEEK ONE

Pray this Way

"This, then, is how you should pray."

Day 1: Like Jesus

Day 2: When You Pray

Day 3: Our Father

Day 4: Your Kingdom

Day 5: Daily Bread

Day 6: Forgive Us

Day 7: Deliver Us

DAY ONE

Like Jesus

Jesus is our perfect, sinless Savior. He paid the price for our sin and took the punishment we deserve. He went to the Cross to free us of our shame, and He removed all wrath and judgment from us. He covers us in righteousness and gives us new life the moment we surrender our life to Him. Through Jesus, we are washed in God's grace, wrapped in God's love, and filled with God's peace. Our Savior guarantees our entrance into the Kingdom of Heaven **(Colossians 2:14)**.

Jesus is our sovereign Lord and mighty King. He rules in authority over all of creation. He reigns supreme over your life and mine. He extends His scepter of justice. He is seated at the right hand of the Father, far above every power and dominion **(Ephesians 1:20-22)**.

Jesus is our faithful friend. He has made known to us everything He learned from His Father **(John 15:15)**.

Jesus is our faultless example. He demonstrated how to love and serve one another **(John 13:15)**. He taught us that true righteousness involves more than our actions—it springs from the deepest recesses of our hearts. Jesus exhibited obedience to His Heavenly Father. He showed us how to live a life of prayer.

We'll look deeper into Jesus' prayer life and gather inspiration for ourselves.

Jesus is a member of the Holy Trinity—Father, Son, and Holy Spirit. He is the exact representation of God. He left the glory of Heaven's Throne Room in pursuit of you and me. He came to win our hearts back and restore our relationship with the Father.

"Who, being in very nature God, did not consider equality with God something to be used to his own advantage; ⁷ rather, he made himself nothing by taking the very nature of a servant, being made in human likeness. ⁸ And being found in appearance as a man, he humbled himself by becoming obedient to death—even

death on a cross! ⁹ Therefore God exalted him to the highest place and gave him the name that is above every name, ¹⁰ that at the name of Jesus every knee should bow, in heaven and on earth and under the earth, ¹¹ and every tongue acknowledge that Jesus Christ is Lord, to the glory of God the Father." Philippians 2:6-11

Jesus knew that to fulfill His purpose here on earth, He had to stay connected to His Heavenly Father. Throughout His time walking this planet (that He created long ago), He carried an ongoing conversation. Prayer was His lifeline—it brought Him peace, it kept Him focused, it filled Him with strength, it was an expression of His gratitude, it was a release for His sorrow.

Let's look at a handful of verses to get a better glimpse of Jesus' connection to the Father. And then we will begin to follow in His prayerful footsteps.

1. Please read the following verses and make note of what you learn about Jesus' prayer life.

    - Mark 1:35

    - Luke 5:16

    - Luke 6:12

"When all the people were being baptized, Jesus was baptized too. And as he was praying, heaven was opened ²² and the Holy Spirit descended on him in bodily form like a dove. And a voice came from heaven:

'You are my Son, whom I love; with you I am well pleased.'" Luke 3:21-22

I'm sure you noticed that prayer was a regular part of Jesus' life. He prayed in public **(John 11:41-42)**. He prayed often and alone. He withdrew from the crowd and sought quiet time with His Father. He prayed during the day and through the watches of the night. He prayed at His baptism in the Jordan River. He prayed during the forty days and nights He spent alone in the desert. He prayed before His earthly ministry began. His prayers invited the blessing and power of God.

"Pray continually." 1 Thessalonians 5:17

2. How often do you withdraw from the noise and seek refuge with the Lord? It's easier to hear Him in the quiet.

3. Do you have a special spot where you meet uninterrupted with God? It's truly a blessing to give Him your undivided attention.

4. Do you regularly converse with Him throughout the day? He is a great companion.

5. Do you talk to Him on those nights when your mind is running wild? If He can hold the moon and stars in place, He can surely handle your problems **(Psalm 4:8)**.

6. Do you remember to pause and pray during the big moments of your life? Do you pray in preparation for what lies ahead? God is present in it all.

> "On my bed I remember you; I think of you through the watches of the night.
>
> ⁷ Because you are my help, I sing in the shadow of your wings." Psalm 63:6-7

Today your assignment is to consciously work on your responses to these questions. Withdraw from the noise, find a quiet spot, converse with the Lord, turn your concerns into prayers, come to the Father in the moment, and in anticipation of what awaits down the road.

> "I call on you, my God, for you will answer me; turn your ear to me and hear my prayer. ⁷ Show me the wonders of your great love, you who save by your right hand those who take refuge in you from their foes." Psalm 17:6-7

Use this Psalm as a prompt for your own prayer. Write your prayer here and then speak it aloud. It will encourage your heart and bless the Lord. Jot down anything that comes to mind—your worship and praises, your cares and concerns, your doubts and questions. (Use a notebook or journal if you need more space.)

God is waiting and He is listening:

My God,

Amen.

DAY TWO

When You Pray

For some people prayer feels completely natural—the words effortlessly flow from their mouths. They confidently pray out loud and on the spot. Their lives are characterized by prayer. For others, prayer is a bit uncomfortable and foreign. It's a source of guilt—not praying enough, or properly. God wants us to know there is no perfect way to come to Him in prayer—that is a pressure that we unnecessarily put on ourselves. Prayer is the act of conversing with our Lord and Savior, our Heavenly Father from above. He may have created the heavens and the earth, and He may be seated on His Heavenly Throne, but He is very, very, near to each one of us. He is acutely aware of every detail of our lives. He is not far off, but intimately close to everyone who calls on His Holy Name. Prayer is our lifeline to God; it aligns our hearts to His; it lightens our loads and eases our burdens. Prayer honors God as Lord of our lives. Prayer is a time to rejoice with the Lord and thank Him for all our blessings, and it is an opportunity to bring Him our cares and concerns. Prayer is surely a privilege we don't want to miss out on.

When Jesus, God in the flesh walked this earth, He taught His followers many things about the Kingdom of Heaven. One day while talking with His disciples, they asked Him to teach them how to pray **(Luke 11:1)**. They had seen Him pray on numerous occasions and noticed something remarkably different. And they wanted it for themselves. Jesus is our perfect example in everything, and among those things is prayer. I want to know Jesus' answer, and I'm sure you do too!

In **Matthew 6:5-13** we find record of Jesus' response. He first told His disciples what not to do and then shared a template they could use in guiding their prayers. (We are Jesus' disciples too, so His teachings apply to us.) Please read the following passage and listen to Jesus' words (I have included the NIV):

"And when you pray, do not be like the hypocrites, for they love to pray standing in the synagogues and on the street corners to be seen by others. Truly I tell you, they have received their reward in full. ⁶ But when you pray, go into your room, close the door and pray to your Father, who is unseen. Then your Father, who sees what is done in secret, will reward you. ⁷ And when you pray, do not keep on babbling like pagans, for they think they will be heard because of their many

words. *⁸ Do not be like them, for your Father knows what you need before you ask him.*

⁹ This, then, is how you should pray:

'Our Father in heaven,
hallowed be your name,
¹⁰ your kingdom come, your will be done,
on earth as it is in heaven.
¹¹ Give us today our daily bread.
¹² And forgive us our debts,
as we also have forgiven our debtors.
¹³ And lead us not into temptation,
but deliver us from the evil one.
*For Yours is the kingdom and the power and the glory forever.
Amen.'"

(The last line is included in the NKJV)

1. Go back over the passage and underline all the phrases that begin "when you pray..."

2. In verses **6:5-8**, what does Jesus say we shouldn't do?

3. Tucked in verse **6:6**, what does Jesus encourage us to do?

4. How do His words address the motives of our hearts?

5. What affirmation do we find in verse **6:8**? What does this mean to you personally?

Prayer is all about fellowship between God and us. We don't need to impress anyone else. Jesus warned His followers against praying meaningless repetitions. We don't need to babble on and on, hoping to get God's attention or educate Him on our situation—He knows it all, but wants us to come to Him regardless. Prayer should be so characteristic of our lives that it's our natural response whether anyone else is watching or not. Praying with others is wonderful, but prayer in private is a precious time of being one-on-one with the Lord. Prayer is truly a matter of the heart.

After addressing the *do's* and *don'ts* of prayer in verses **6:5-8**, Jesus goes on to share an example of the themes we are to pray about. The verses in **Matthew 6:9-13** and in **Luke 11:2-4** are referred to as *The Lord's Prayer*—after all, He is the One who taught us to pray it. This simple prayer is beautiful on its own and is often recited word for word as an expression of our sincere devotion. (You may already do this, and that's truly lovely.) But Jesus wants to make sure our prayer life is personal, alive, and authentic; He doesn't want us to fall into the pattern of reading His prayer by rote. Jesus' phrases are intended to be a wonderful springboard for all the topics that He highlights for us—worship, thanksgiving, our daily needs, forgiveness, protection, and praise. Memorizing Jesus' prayer is helpful in guiding the course of our own personalized sentiments.

The various versions of the Bible give us further insight as to Jesus' intention for the use of His prayer.

NIV: *This then is how you should pray…*

NKJV: *In this manner, therefore, pray…*

NLT: *Pray like this…*

NASB: *Pray then, in this way…*

ESV: *Pray then, like this…*

Jesus never said, *pray exactly like this, and only like this*. In fact, throughout the four Gospels we see that Jesus used many other words as well when speaking to His Heavenly Father. Of course, we can pray *The Lord's Prayer* verbatim, but like with any other conversation, it's important that we *also* share what is going on currently in our hearts, minds, and lives. It's also vital that our worship is resoundingly alive and genuine in the moment. Most of the time our awe and reverence of God is so uncontainable that it's hard to fully capture in one phrase. Although, we are sometimes left speechless!

Before we look at each of Jesus' prompts, let's first take a few moments to appreciate and memorize His prayer as a whole.

In your own hand, use this space to write out *The Lord's Prayer* exactly as Matthew recorded it and just the way Jesus taught it. Then reread His words a few times to yourself, meditating on them as you do. Finally, read them aloud as a prayer to your Heavenly Father.

Memorize this prayer and tuck it into your heart.

DAY THREE

Our Father

"'Our Father in heaven, hallowed be your name."

Over the last two days we have laid a firm foundation for our prayers. We looked at Jesus as our example and we familiarized ourselves with His teaching on prayer. For the remainder of this week, we will look more closely at *The Lord's Prayer*, one verse at a time, and then we will put it into practice. The first line alone holds so much gravity in such a short phrase. We are immediately faced with the reality of who God is. He rules in complete authority from His Throne Room in Heaven; He is sovereign over all of creation. The earth is His mere footstool; He can hold all the seas in the palm of His hand. **(Isaiah 66:1; 40:12)** And yet He is close to every one of us. He reigns from on high but bends down low for our sake. He is attentive and involved with every single detail of our lives. He calls us into a personal relationship with Himself. He is our loving Father.

God is the perfect blend of power and love. This means we can confidently pray to Him about anything and everything. If He held all the power that's in existence but was unloving and unkind, we would be afraid to approach Him. If He were kind and loving but powerless to help us, then we would not be inclined to turn to Him in our time of need. Since He is both powerful and loving, we know that He not only desires to help us, but He is fully able to do so. His love is higher and deeper and wider than we can possibly imagine. In case you ever doubt it—the Cross is our proof **(Ephesians 3:18)**. Nothing can ever separate us from His love—not life, death, or anything in-between **(Romans 8:37-39)**. His power is mightier than we can begin to fathom. He heals the sick, He raises the dead, and He casts out demons **(Matthew 4:23-24)**. He calms the raging seas; He stills the storms in you and me **(Matthew 8:26)**.

Stepping into God's Presence, we can't help but be overcome with awe and reverence. There is no one like Him and there never will be. God is God: The King of kings, the Lord of lords, the Almighty God, the Prince of Peace, the Alpha and Omega, the Beginning and the End. The heavens declare the splendor of His glory **(Psalm 19:1)**. His Name alone is to be hallowed and praised.

"LORD, our Lord, how majestic is your name in all the earth! You have set your glory in the heavens. ² Through the praise of children and infants you have established a stronghold against your enemies, to silence the foe and the avenger. ³ When I consider your heavens, the work of your fingers, the moon and the stars, which you have set in place, ⁴ what is mankind that you are mindful of them, human beings that you care for them?" Psalm 8:1-4

1. Take a moment to read **Psalm 8:1-4** aloud. Meditate on the words as you do so. Afterwards write down any impression that God lays on your heart.

Using the Scriptures and the impressions they sparked, record your own prayer in the space provided. Then read it aloud to your Heavenly Father. Use Jesus' prompt to get you started:

Our Father in Heaven, hallowed be Your name,

Amen.

DAY FOUR

Your Kingdom

"Your kingdom come, your will be done, on earth as it is in heaven."

Jesus' prayer prompts build upon each other, one naturally leading into the next. Knowing that our Heavenly Father reigns from His throne in Heaven above and that He is all-powerful loving, kind, and just, makes us long for His Kingdom to take over the earth. Jesus came once to bring us salvation—freedom from our sins and from the threat of death. We have new life through His death on the Cross. Jesus was three days in the grave and then He rose victorious. His resurrection is the crux of our faith. We have the promise that death is not the end for us; it is just our transition into eternity in Heaven. Jesus was the first to experience resurrection and someday we will experience it too. Before Jesus left this planet and ascended back to Heaven, He gave His solemn promise to return for us someday. This will be the Second Coming of Christ **(Revelation 1:5-8)**.

When Jesus returns, He will set up His Heavenly Kingdom here on earth. He will dwell among His people forever. His glory will radiate throughout the city as bright as day. Sin and sorrow, shame and regret, pain and suffering will have no place in His Holy City **(Revelation 21:4)**. There will be only abundant blessing, constant peace, overflowing joy, sincere love, and the presence of our Lord. What a beautiful hope that awaits our future. Our prayers confess our desire for His Kingdom to come soon.

Our prayers also recognize our desire for His Kingdom to come alive in and around us, here and now. We instantly become citizens in the Kingdom of God when we place our faith in Jesus as Lord and Savior of our lives **(Philippians 3:20)**. Heaven becomes our hope and our home, and a new longing for righteousness takes over. We yearn for God's righteousness to reign on the earth, and we hunger and thirst for His righteousness to rule in our hearts **(Matthew 5:6)**. We want His will to be done in every single matter. Praying for His will to be done on earth as it is in Heaven, aligns our hearts with His will. God promises that if we hunger and thirst for righteousness in our lives, He will surely respond by filling us.

"But our citizenship is in heaven. And we eagerly await a Savior from there, the Lord Jesus Christ, [21] who, by the power that enables him to bring everything under his control, will transform our lowly bodies so that they will be like his glorious body."

Philippians 3:20-21

1. Read **Revelation 1:5-8** for yourself. How does the promise of Jesus' return give you hope for the future?

2. How has it instilled a longing for righteousness to rule the earth now?

3. Describe the hunger and thirst it creates in you.

Write a brief prayer asking God to satisfy you.

O, Lord, Your kingdom come, your will be done, on earth as it is in heaven,

Amen.

DAY FIVE

Daily Bread

"Give us today our daily bread."

God is Creator of heaven and earth, and He is Creator of you and me. He sustains the universe both day and night, ushering the moon across the sky and calling the stars out each night. He causes the sun to rise every morning and to set each twilight. He keeps the world spinning; He causes rain to fall, seeds to sprout, and seasons to come and go. The Lord God Almighty is both Creator and Sustainer. He offers to sustain us as we walk with Him one day at a time. He is more than capable of sustaining every part of our being—body, mind, spirit, and heart. He knows precisely how He knit us together, He remembers every loving stitch. He has recorded every day of our lives in His Book. He knows exactly what we need at any given moment. He sees our heart, He knows our struggles, He is aware of our circumstances, needs, and desires. There is no better place or person to turn than to our Faithful Provider. No matter where we are or what we are going through, He is always very near to us **(Psalm 139:1-18)**.

God provides in countless ways—He provides salvation through His Divine Gift of Grace; He provides knowledge and wisdom when we ask and seek it. He provides healing for our wounded bodies, and He mends our broken hearts. He provides strength for the weary; He provides counsel and guidance for our journey. He provides comfort and peace when we rest in His presence; He provides endless love to fill all the longings of our heart. He provides nourishment for our bodies and spiritual food for our souls. In **John 6:35** we read, *"Jesus declared, 'I am the bread of life.'"* He shows us the way to escape temptation. He provides refuge when we need safety. He provides all the gifts, talents, treasures, and resources we need to bless others and glorify His Name **(2 Peter 1:1-4)**.

Daily bread can represent so many things. Depending on the day and what we are facing, our prayer for *daily bread* will take on a different meaning. It can even change from morning to night. Our needs can range and shift from physical, to emotional, or mental, or spiritual. We can cling to the wonderful promises, confident that God is sufficient to meet them all. He satisfies the needs that we bring before Him for ourselves, and those that we bring on behalf of others.

"Sing out your thanks to the LORD; sing praises to our God with a harp. ⁸ He covers the heavens with clouds, provides rain for the earth, and makes the grass grow in mountain pastures. ⁹ He gives food to the wild animals and feeds the young ravens when they cry." Psalm 147:7-9 NLT

1. Read **Psalm 147:1-20** in your Bible. List the verbs describing God's action in the lives of His children. How does this encourage your heart?

2. What needs do you have to bring to your Creator and Sustainer today?

Now turn your answer to the previous question into a prayer:

Dear Lord, Give us today our daily bread,

Amen.

DAY SIX

Forgive Us

"And forgive us our debts, as we also have forgiven our debtors."

This may be the most challenging out of all of Jesus' prayer prompts. Admittedly, the first half of the plea is easier to profess than the latter part. Forgiveness from the Lord is greatly appreciated and desired. And we need it fresh every day. Our sins are forgiven, and our slate is wiped clean the moment we accept Jesus as our Lord and Savior. We now stand before God clothed in the righteousness of Christ, enrobed in pure white, spotless linen. Jesus' perfection is imputed to us. God declares us not guilty. Although we can confidently enter Heaven's Gates, we will still stand before the Lord's judgment seat and give an account for our actions **(Romans 14:10-12)**. Jesus' sacrifice covers all our sins—past, present, and future. But I'm sure you've noticed, that although God declares you innocent, there are still days and moments when you fall flat on your face. And He asks us to deal with those instances when they do come.

Our first confession is one of faith: *"If you declare with your mouth, 'Jesus is Lord,' and believe in your heart that God raised him from the dead, you will be saved."* **(Romans 10:9)**. After that, confession should become a regular part of our lives—not to save us, but to continually purify and refine us. Every time we sin, by saying something we shouldn't or doing something harmful, a barrier goes up between God and us. In **Genesis 3:6-10**, we read about how sin became the hedge between Adam and Eve and God—they literally hid in the bushes. The couple formerly enjoyed an unhindered relationship with the Lord. They regularly and freely walked and talked with Him in the Garden of Eden. Once sin entered in, regret overtook them, and they tried to hide their shame. They hid from God, their loving Creator. This is what we hope to avoid. By openly confessing our sins on a consistent basis we don't give them a chance to bring division. Instead, we share them with God right away so He can cover our shame and help us deal with the consequences. Adam and Eve made a feeble attempt at covering their own sin—fig leaves that would eventually dry out and crumble. God on the other hand provided an animal sacrifice and covered them with skins, which were much longer lasting. By the way, this is a foreshadowing of God providing the perfect sacrifice of His Son to completely cover our sin and shame forever.

The second half of Jesus' prayer doesn't come quite so easy and that's why Jesus gives us a little extra nudge. Remembering the grace that God shows us should motivate us to show grace as well. No one is perfect—that's why Jesus came.

"For if you forgive other people when they sin against you, your heavenly Father will also forgive you. ⁱ⁵ But if you do not forgive others their sins, your Father will not forgive your sins." Matthew 6:14-15

1. Read **Psalm 32:1-11** and encounter the blessings of confession. Is there something you need to confess and ask God forgiveness for?

2. Is there someone you need to forgive and release to God?

Pray now and confess your sins. God will gladly forgive you. *His mercies are new every day.* Pray also that God would help you forgive anyone who needs your forgiveness. This is the key to freeing your own heart from bitterness.

Merciful Father, forgive us our debts, as we also have forgiven our debtors,

Amen.

DAY SEVEN

Deliver Us

"And lead us not into temptation, but deliver us from the evil one."

Adam and Eve were the first people to be tempted and we've been feeling the repercussions of their decision ever since. Satan had been hiding in the wings waiting for the moment to spring his deception. God had told the couple they could eat of any tree in the Garden of Eden with one important exception: **Genesis 2:16-17**, *"And the LORD God commanded the man, "You are free to eat from any tree in the garden;* **17** *but you must not eat from the tree of the knowledge of good and evil, for when you eat from it you will certainly die."* Because of their disobedience to God's command, they were driven from the Garden and had consequences to bear. But even in their discipline, we see God's grace on display. Besides the *Tree of the Knowledge of Good and Evil*, there was another tree from which they had not eaten—*The Tree of Life*. If they had eaten from this tree they would have lived forever in their fallen state. God banished them from the Garden and posted an angel with a flaming sword to protect them from further access and eternal separation **(Genesis 3:22-24)**. As God proclaimed judgments, He also promised a Savior who would come and crush Satan's head **(Genesis 3:15)**.

Our sins may not have the same worldwide, historical ramifications and implications as Adam and Eve's, but they still leave their mark—on us and on others. Satan is still prowling around looking for someone to devour and lead astray **(1 Peter 5:8)**, but thankfully God is our Defender. If we draw near to God, He will draw near to us. If we resist the devil, he will flee **(James 4:7-8)**. That's a promise from Scripture!

God has not left us unaware—Scripture warns us over and over again: to pray and prepare, to be alert, to be on guard against all the enemy's schemes. The devil knows our weaknesses and we need to be aware of them too. Put on God's Armor and stand your holy ground **(Ephesians 6:11)**.

Satan is our tempter, but God always provides a way out. We can either give in to temptation or resist it. There is always a choice, but we'd be wise to surrender to the Spirit's prompting. When Satan dangles a carrot, we don't have to bite.

Pray ahead and give it to God in the moment. Pray even under your breath for the strength to overcome and resist. God will deliver you from evil.

"No temptation has overtaken you except what is common to mankind. And God is faithful; he will not let you be tempted beyond what you can bear. But when you are tempted, he will also provide a way out so that you can endure it."

1 Corinthians 10:13

1. **1 Corinthians 10:1-13** warns us against giving in to temptation. What times and circumstances are you most prone to being tempted—either in your words or actions?

2. How do you resist temptation—in Jesus' strength or your own **(Hebrews 2:14-18)**?

Take a moment to write a prayer asking God to help you recognize temptation and to then deliver you from it.

God Almighty, lead us not into temptation, but deliver us from the evil one.

Amen.

"Shout for joy to the LORD, all the earth.

²Worship the LORD with gladness;

come before him with joyful songs.

³Know that the LORD is God.

It is he who made us, and we are his;

we are his people, the sheep of his pasture.

⁴Enter his gates with thanksgiving

and his courts with praise;

give thanks to him and praise his name.

⁵For the LORD is good and his love endures forever;

his faithfulness continues through all generations." Psalm 100:1-5

WEEK TWO

Worship

"Our Father in heaven, hallowed be your name."

Day 1: God is Creator

Day 2: God is Eternal

Day 3: God is Holy

Day 4: God is Love

Day 5: God is Merciful

Day 6: God is Worthy

Day 7: God is Mighty

DAY ONE

God is Creator

"In the beginning God created the heavens and the earth." Genesis 1:1

The Bible opens with the indisputable proclamation that *God created*! Our Creator spoke the heavens and earth into existence with just a word. He separated light from dark, day from night. He set the sun, moon, and stars to shine in the sky. He created the atmosphere that surrounds our planet to protect us from the vast expanse of galaxies. He created the perfect environment for the rest of His creation to survive and thrive. He created dry land and seas that reach the shores; lush plants and fragrant flowers; delicious fruits and diverse vegetables that provide healthy food to eat. He created animals, birds, reptiles, fish, and swimming mammals of all shapes and sizes. God announced that all His creation was *good*. But His crowning creation was His beloved mankind. His crowning creation includes you and me. We were made in His image—the very image of God. We were created to reflect His glory on earth.

Everywhere we look we see evidence that points us to our Creator. Things didn't just pop into being of their own accord, and nothing was accidental. Creation was God's perfect plan. Great attention and intention were paid to every detail. He brought it all into existence according to His perfect will.

Worshipping God begins with recognizing Him as our Creator. He is the architect of all our eye can see and everything beyond our limited scope and view. A wonderful way to find inspiration for our *prayers of worship* is to simply open our eyes and look around us. All of creation testifies to God's glory—the celestial canopy above our heads, the damp grass blades beneath our feet, the grainy sand squishing between our toes. The wide array of flowers with a variety of colors and scents. The varying shades of green on the tree branches as they sway. The invisible wind that brushes past our face. The radiant sun that warms our skin. Snowflakes that gently land on our eyelashes. Taking a walk outside and marveling at nature will surely inspire our praises. If the weather or your circumstances prevent you from going outdoors, you can always watch the seasons slowly approach and fade from the comfort of your home. You might glimpse squirrels scurrying by and birds flitting past, and maybe one will even land on your windowsill to say *hello*.

Besides contemplating the beauty of nature, we find great inspiration for our prayers by considering how God made *us*. We can praise God for the way He masterfully formed our bodies. He made our entire being function together with perfect precision—our heart, lungs, and many other organs that sustain our life. Eyes, ears, nose, and mouth that provide our senses; our skin, hair, and nails; arms and legs, hands and feet. On top of all that He gave us extremely complex brains. And every part works seamlessly together! Amazing!

1. Please read **Genesis 1:1-31** and make note of everything God created and how He brought it into existence.

2. How does nature inspire you to worship the Lord? How about the miracle of life He gave you?

Let's use our God-given breath to praise Him. Turn your observations into a worshipful prayer to your Creator:

Masterful Creator,

Amen.

DAY TWO

God is Eternal

"'I am the Alpha and the Omega,' says the Lord God, 'who is, and who was, and who is to come, the Almighty.'" Revelation 1:8

God's eternal existence confirms Him as Creator. His eternal nature seamlessly overlaps with His holy and almighty character. The essence and sum of all His attributes beautifully weave together, proving that God alone is worthy of our praises. For the next few days, we will continue looking at each characteristic, but for today we'll direct our worship toward *God Eternal*.

God is eternal, outside of history as we know it. The Bible refers to God as the *Ancient of Days* **(Daniel 7)**, and the Scriptures inform us that He is *from ancient days* of which we cannot fathom **(Isaiah 43:13)**. He has no beginning and no end, yet He is the author of all time and space. **Revelation 22:13** proclaims, *"I am the Alpha and the Omega, the First and the Last, the Beginning and the End."* Being outside of the confines of years and seasons, it pleases Him to give us time as a means to mark and punctuate our lives. He has created a time for everything under the sun—birth and death, weeping and laughing, mourning and dancing **(Ecclesiastes 3:1-8)**. He is present with us through it all!

All creation is laid bare and vast before Him. He sees and knows every moment that has occurred in the past and perceives every single second yet to come. Although He is above and beyond every age and era, He is present with each generation. **Exodus 34:5** says, *"Then the LORD came down in the cloud and stood there with him [Moses] and proclaimed His name, the LORD."*

I find it truly remarkable that God is both eternal and He leans down low to involve Himself with our lives. He is not only *aware* of what happened in the past, or in the present, or will come to be in the future; He is also intimately *involved*. The Lord rescues and responds; He is our strength and our hope. He scatters our enemies and reaches out from on high just to bring us comfort. He is our Rock, our Deliverer, our Shield, and our Salvation! It is amazing to think that our Eternal God delights in us and chooses to come near!

God Eternal stepped down from Heaven and was born in a manger. He clothed Himself in human flesh. Jesus is *Emmanuel, God with us*. **(Matthew 1:23)**

1. Please read **Revelation 4:1-11** and note your impression of the scene in Heaven.

2. Now turn to **Psalm 18:1-19** and take in the Lord's words of comfort. How do you feel knowing that God leaves His Temple in Heaven to come and rescue you? **(vs. 18:6, 9, 16)**

Notice how these Scriptures depict God's eternal nature, also how His power and mercy perfectly converge. Although God is eternal, He is also in the moment with you. Use these verses to guide your prayers to *the Lord God Almighty, who was, and is, and is to come* **(Revelation 4:8)**.

Lord God Almighty,

Amen.

DAY THREE

God is Holy

"Exalt the LORD our God and worship at his holy mountain,

for the LORD our God is holy." Psalm 99:9

The word *holy* describes the uniqueness of God. It means to be *set apart, distinct, incomparable, different from the world, distinguished, sacred*. God is most definitely holy—He is so very unlike you and me. Thank goodness! He is not tempted by sin, He is not threatened by death, He is unruffled by troubles, He is never consumed with worry or fear. Pain is not an issue; old age is not a thing. He is unaffected by the concerns that affect all of mankind. He is sinless, perfect, eternal, sovereign, all-knowing, all-sufficient, omnipresent—none of which can be said of people. God is above and beyond and greater than man. **Exodus 15:11** poses this rhetorical question: *"Who among the gods is like you, LORD? Who is like you—majestic in holiness, awesome in glory, working wonders?"* The answer is no one, that's who!

God is unlike humans in that He never changes His mind and its impossible for Him to lie **(1 Samuel 15:29)**. Everything in heaven and on earth is His; He is *exalted as head over all* **(1 Chronicles 29:11)**. His glory radiates throughout the heavens and fills the earth below. His Name is to be praised above all names. **Psalm 29:2** exhorts us, *"Ascribe to the LORD the glory due his name; worship the LORD in the splendor of his holiness."*

Aren't you glad that you aren't relying on a god who is vulnerable and prone to the same weaknesses, doubts, and wishy-washiness that you are? I sure am! He doesn't change like the shifting shadows on the pavement as the sun peaks and fades; He isn't tossed to and fro by the current or the waves. He isn't blown this way and that with the cultural winds of change. Emotions never get the better of Him. He is stable, steadfast, and sure; He is trustworthy and righteous. His ways are above our ways; His wisdom is greater than the smartest of minds. The list goes on and on regarding how God's holiness makes Him different from us.

Although God is holy on a whole other level, we are called to be holy as well. Besides being holy, God is also our loving Father. God wants His children to aim for holiness so that we represent Him accurately while residing on this planet. His Kingdom is one of holy righteousness, and that is the Kingdom to which we truly belong. Jesus exhorted us to be *in the world but not of it*. We are called to a life of holiness—to be separate and distinct as Christ-followers **(John 17:15-17)**.

Living by God's Word and aligning our lives to His will sanctifies and sets us apart for His purpose.

1. Please read **Exodus 20:1-21** to see God's Laws. They are intended to help us align our lives to His holiness. You may recognize these as *The Ten Commandments*. The first few commandments prescribe holiness in our relationship with God. The others detail the commandments for holy living in relation to each other. (See **Matthew 22:37-40** for Jesus' summarization of the Law.) How do these commandments better help you understand the holiness of God, and what He desires from you?

Take a moment to pray and praise God for His holiness. Thank Him for being unique, incomparable, distinct, and sacred. Ask Him to help you be holy too.

Dear Holy Father,

Amen.

DAY FOUR

God is Love

"Whoever does not love does not know God, because God is love." 1 John 4:8

If you ever wonder what love looks like, just remember the Cross of Calvary. God gave His Son to take the punishment that our sins deserve **(John 3:16)**. Jesus' outstretched arms reveal the extremes that God went to in order to bring us into a relationship with Himself. This love is beyond my comprehension—but I am extremely and forever grateful for it! God's very essence is love, and every bit of love flows directly from Him. *Our* capacity and willingness to love often depends on our emotions, or is based on our satisfaction with the other person. God's love on the other hand, is founded on His unchanging, unconditional commitment, not on our behavior. He *is* love—the goodness and purity of love are all wrapped up in Him. His love follows us all the days of our lives—it pursues, woos, and invites **(Psalm 23:6)**. It forgives and sees the best in us. His love restores and redeems what was lost. His love floods our hearts and invigorates our spirits. God's love is great and unfailing. It is extravagantly sacrificial, whether we deserve it or not.

1 Corinthians 13:4-8 paints a vivid picture of God's love for us:

"Love is patient, love is kind. It does not envy, it does not boast, it is not proud. [5] It does not dishonor others, it is not self-seeking, it is not easily angered, it keeps no record of wrongs. [6] Love does not delight in evil but rejoices with the truth. [7] It always protects, always trusts, always hopes, always perseveres. [8] Love never fails."

This is how God loves us. His love leaves no room for insecurity or fear—He will not reject us **(1 John 4:18)**. His love is utterly perfect in absolutely every way. It never leaves us wanting but satisfies all the needs and desires of our heart. God delights in being the One we turn to, the One we share our hearts with, both our joys and concerns. Too often our affections are misplaced and unrequited; God is always a safe choice with whom to entrust them. The next time you feel unwanted or unloved, run into the loving arms of the Lord—He is waiting to embrace you!

I have performed a couple of marriage ceremonies—for my sister and brother-in-law, and for my aunt and uncle—using these verses from **1 Corinthians 13**. As I read the Scriptures, I made sure to emphasize that this kind of love is only possible with God working in us and flowing through us.

1. For a clear display of God's love, please read **John 3:16-17**. What does this love mean for you?

2. Please read **1 John 4:7-21** to hear the Lord's exhortations for us in response to His love. What response does the Lord require?

Now comes the time for praising God. Praise Him for His unconditional love. Thank Him that it never fails. Ask Him to fill you with His love and help you to overflow more freely.

My Loving and Faithful God,

Amen.

DAY FIVE

God is Merciful

"But in your great mercy you did not put an end to them or abandon them, for you are a gracious and merciful God." Nehemiah 9:31

When Adam and Eve took a bite of the forbidden fruit on that day long ago in the Garden of Eden, God could have said, *I warned you, too bad, now you get to deal with the consequences on your own*. But He didn't! He sacrificed animals on their behalf and made coverings of skin to hide their nakedness and cover their shame. He gave them promises to cling to—He would send a Savior to pay the price for their transgression and to save all of mankind from death and sin **(Genesis 3:15, 21)**. Generations later when the nation of Israel turned its back on God, forsook His righteous ways, worshipped worthless idols, and were taken captive to faraway foreign lands, The Lord God Almighty could have shaken His head and said, *you got what you deserve—now live with it*. But He didn't! He sent prophets to the people, exhorting repentance over and over again. God drew the people's hearts toward Himself, and He restored them to the Promised Land **(Daniel 1:1-2, Ezra 1, Nehemiah 2)**. God is a covenant keeping God and He never breaks His promises. He sent His Son Jesus Christ to redeem humanity just as He had said He would, and He delivered His beloved Israel according to His covenant **(John 3:16-18 and Genesis 15:18)**. Yes, God is merciful indeed to those who turn to Him!

God is merciful not just with people of the past, but with you and me also. He doesn't give us what we deserve—He refrains from judgment and withholds His wrath. The moment we place our faith in Jesus and proclaim Him as Lord and Savior, God forgives our sins and removes them from us as far as the east is from the west **(Psalm 103:12)**. Amen! His mercy withholds punishment, and His grace pours out lavish acceptance. There is nothing we can humanly do to deserve this extravagance—we merely accept His gift by faith and turn our lives around in repentance. Being saved by His mercy compels us to pivot away from our sin and move toward holiness in complete surrender. God's Word says, *"Be holy, as I AM holy."* **(1 Peter 1:14-16 and Leviticus 11:44-45)**

Worship, gratitude, honor, and holiness are our instinctual responses.

1. Please open your Bible to **Ephesians 2:1-10** and read about the Lord's great mercy. Make note of all the blessings we incur because of His rich mercy.

2. How does God's generous mercy impact you personally?

"The LORD lives! Praise be to my Rock! Exalted be God my Savior!" Psalm 18:46

Reflect on the Lord's mercy and grace and write a prayer of worship in response. Thank Him for your new life in Christ and ask Him to help you live for Him in return.

My Merciful Savior,

Amen.

DAY SIX

God is Worthy

"You are worthy, our Lord and God, to receive glory and honor and power, for you created all things, and by your will they were created and have their being."

Revelation 4:11

God alone is worthy of our worship. He deserves all honor, glory, and praise. Far too often though, we bow down before gods of lesser making and means **(Deuteronomy 11:16)**. Our adoration and worship go to our relationships, to success, to power, to money, to other people such as spouses, children, pastors, politicians, or celebrities whom we put on pedestals **(2 Kings 17:41)**. We place all our confidence, security, hopes and dreams upon them. And when those people and things don't live up to our expectations and topple from high places, we act surprised. Nothing and no one will ever compare to the Lord, and He commands that we do not worship idols or any other gods alongside Him **(Exodus 23:24)**. He alone can completely satisfy. He alone is sufficient for all our needs. He alone created all things, and He sustains everything in existence. He has triumphed over sin and death. He has paid the price for our sins and unlocked the chains that formerly held us in bondage—He has set us free! The same cannot be said about anything or anyone else we could possibly place our faith in.

The angels gather round His glorious throne both day and night, to sing His endless praises. The demons are under God's ultimate authority and shudder at the sound of His Name. Someday He will pronounce judgment upon the sin that is rampant on the earth and on Satan and all his followers. He will justify and redeem those whose names have been recorded in His Book of Life—we will be forever welcomed into the gates of Heaven **(Revelation 3:5)**.

Jesus is the Lamb of God who takes away the sins of the world. He is over and above everything—it's all under His dominion **(Ephesians 1:21-23)**!

Stop searching, cease striving. Bow before the Lord in worship and you will find your heart is lifted!

"Then I heard every creature in heaven and on earth and under the earth and on the sea, and all that is in them, saying: 'To him who sits on the throne and to the Lamb be praise and honor and glory and power, for ever and ever!'" Revelations 5:13

1. Please refer to **Revelation 5:1-14** and read more about the Lord's worthiness. (Jesus is both the Lion and the Lamb.) Write out verse **5:9** and record what this means to you. The scroll represents God's judgment upon the earth and all those who have rejected Him.

2. How does worship in Heaven inspire your own worship? We literally join in the heavenly chorus of praise.

Worship the Lord for being worthy of all praise. Express your gratitude to God for rescuing you from judgment and including you in His Kingdom.

To Him who sits on the Throne and to the Lamb, You alone are worthy of praise,

Amen.

DAY SEVEN

God is Mighty

"The Mighty One, God, the LORD, speaks and summons the earth from the rising of the sun to where it sets." Psalm 50:1

When you think of the word *mighty,* who or what comes to mind? Superheroes like Superman and the Hulk? Everyday heroes such as firefighters and police officers? Or is it stormy seas, hurricane winds, raging wildfires, volcanic eruptions, and magnitude 10 earthquakes? Although something different may pop into each of our thoughts, we all most likely equate *might* with bravery, power, and strength. There is no one stronger that our Lord God Almighty. He can calm the stormy seas or whip them into a frenzy; He can douse a flame with rain from the sky or fan the flame even higher. There is nothing too big or too difficult for God to tackle. When David fought the giant Goliath, it was not by his own strength that he emerged as a conqueror. He knew the battle belonged to the Lord and trusted that God would give Him victory **(Psalm 24:8; 1 Samuel 17)**. And yes, God most certainly did—with the power of God working in and through him, David brought down the giant with just a sling and a stone. The armor that the soldiers offered him to wear did not fit, so it appeared that he went against the giant quite vulnerable and unprotected. But David wore the Armor of God **(Ephesians 6:11)**!

The *might* of God moves mountains—both the hillsides that grow dense forests, and the obstacles that crop up in our lives. God Almighty parted the Red Sea with a wind so powerful that Moses and the Israelites crossed over on dry land **(Exodus 14:29-31)**. He protected them from the ensuing Egyptians and brought them into the Promised Land. He gave the Israelites success as they overtook the pagan nations around them. God even brought down the walls of the fortified city of Jericho through the peoples' worship and praises. They didn't have to lift a weapon or even a finger. They just lifted their voices in shouts of victory! God is mighty!

When we walk with the Lord God Almighty, He gives us victory too. He causes walls to fall, prison doors to fling open, chains to break; the things that formerly held us captive no longer have a hold or control over us.

Ephesians 1:19-20 tells us, *"His incomparably great power for us who believe. That power is the same as the mighty strength [20] he exerted when he raised Christ from the dead and seated him at his right hand in the heavenly realms..."*

That is a lot of mighty power! The same power that God the Father exhibited when raising Christ from the dead, is the same power at work for, in, and through us! Resurrection power—He brings life to every area of our lives if we choose to believe and receive it! How about that for a confidence booster!

"Finally be strong in the Lord's mighty power." Ephesians 6:10

1. Please read **Ephesians 1:15-23.** How does knowing God and the hope He promises, help strengthen you? Is He your fortress in times of trouble?

2. Are you living in the reality of God's mighty power, which is at work for and in you? Explain.

Write a prayer of worship to God Almighty. Thank Him for His power which works to save you. Ask Him to help you walk in confidence based on His power *in* you.

Mighty One, God my Lord,

Amen.

"Good and upright is the LORD;

therefore he instructs sinners in his ways.

⁹ He guides the humble in what is right

and teaches them his way.

¹⁰ All the ways of the LORD are loving and faithful

toward those who keep the demands of his covenant.

¹¹ For the sake of your name, LORD,

forgive my iniquity, though it is great." Psalm 25:8-11

WEEK THREE

Submission

"Your Kingdom Come, Your Will Be Done."

Day 1: God's Authority

Day 2: Holy Spirit Come

Day 3: Asking for Guidance

Day 4: Seeking God's Will

Day 5: Trusting His Plan

Day 6: Immediate Obedience

Day 7: Complete Surrender

DAY ONE

God's Authority

Recognizing God's supreme authority in this world ushers us to a position of humility and leads to our submission. Our complete surrender opens the door for the Lord to pour abundant blessing into our lives. It is a joy and a privilege to submit to the Lord—He is not harsh; He is loving, good, kind, and gracious. He rules in sovereign authority and reigns with perfect justice. His Kingdom is over all the kingdoms of the earth, past, present, and future **(Ephesians 1:21)**. His Lordship is above every king, president, dictator, and earthly ruler. He is all-powerful and is in command over every angel and demon. At His glorious Name every knee will someday bow in reverence **(Philippians 2:9-11)**. I am so eternally grateful to have been invited and accepted into His Heavenly Dwelling where you and I will reside forever. Submitting to God's authority begins with recognizing our own spiritual lacking—our deficit of righteousness and desperate need for a Savior from above. Once we recognize this need and call out to Jesus, we are assured of our entrance into the Kingdom of Heaven. Becoming a child of God then makes us aware of our sin and this causes us to mourn our flawed condition. God is so good though; He meets our mourning with His gracious comfort. He welcomes us despite ourselves, and He cleans us up and gets us moving in the right direction. We find comfort in knowing that our sins have been removed and we have been washed clean. That is an amazing assurance to me! And I'm sure it is for you too! The word *meek* is not usually thought of as a positive attribute—it's often associated with being a doormat. But that is *not* how the Bible applies it. *Meek* as used by Jesus in the following verses, describes someone who exercises their strength, but yields it to God's control. Jesus promises that *the meek*—those who submit to the Father's authority in their lives—*will inherit the earth*. You may not want to inherit the earth in its current broken condition, but someday God is going to renew it. It will be perfect, beautiful, and untainted by sin. It will then be a treasure worth inheriting! Submission also requires that we lay down our sinful pursuits, passions, and desires. Rather, we must seek the things of God. Our hunger and thirst for His righteousness will be met with a filling that leads to overflowing. Surrender to God admits reliance on Him. It depends on His strength, power, and protection. It confesses Him as King of kings. Submitting to the Lord is not oppressive; it carries abundant peace and freedom **(Psalm 37:11)**.

Jesus said:

"Blessed are the poor in spirit, for theirs is the kingdom of heaven.

⁴ Blessed are those who mourn, for they will be comforted.

⁵ Blessed are the meek, for they will inherit the earth.

⁶ Blessed are those who hunger and thirst for righteousness, for they will be filled."

Matthew 5:3-6

1. Read **Matthew 5:1-12** to hear who Jesus calls blessed, and the blessings He pours out. What does submission to God's authority mean to you?

2. Would you say you have fully surrendered to Him?

Submit your heart and life to God's authority now. Find comfort, peace, and satisfaction waiting for you.
King of kings, Lord of lords,

Amen.

DAY TWO

Holy Spirit Come

God is the Giver of all the best gifts! Every gift He gives is perfect, it always fits, and exchanging it is out of the question **(James 1:17)**. There is nothing better! First, He gives us the gift of salvation through His Son Jesus Christ! Secondly, He gives us the gift of His Holy Spirit who seals us as His beloved possession **(2 Corinthians 1:22; Ephesians 1:13)**. The moment we say *yes* to Jesus, the Holy Spirit comes to dwell in our hearts, and He brings many blessings with Him. He seals and then He fills us! **Ephesians 1:3** says, *"Praise be to the God and Father of our Lord Jesus Christ, who has blessed us in the heavenly realms with every spiritual blessing in Christ."* **2 Peter 1:3** affirms our blessings and lets us know the reason they are given: *"His divine power has given us everything we need for a godly life through our knowledge of him who called us by his own glory and goodness."* God provides everything we need for godly living—that includes steering clear of sin, pursuing His purpose, and glorifying His Name with our lives.

When the Holy Spirit comes to reside in our hearts He ushers in peace, hope, and joy along with Him. He provides comfort amid our trials and tribulations. He reminds us of Jesus' teachings when our minds start to wander **(John 14:26)**. He convicts us of sin and leads us in God's way everlasting. The Holy Spirit also comes bearing delightful and useful packages called *spiritual gifts* **(1 Corinthians 12:1-31)**. Yes, even more gifts—which are to be used to benefit and build up the church and bless everyone we encounter. The Holy Spirit is a supernatural, gracious gift from God above; we must submit to His purpose and leading in our lives daily. God's Holy Spirit only ever leads us to places of more blessing; we can trust Him completely. He always has our best interest at heart—His goal is to grow us more and more into the likeness of Jesus **(Romans 8:29)**. I like that purpose!

As the Holy Spirit works in our hearts, minds, and lives, He may show us things that we'd rather not see, He may reveal a plan we'd rather not follow, or exhort us in ways we'd rather not hear. But it is always in our best interest to heed His voice and quiet nudges. When we ignore Him, we may get too close to danger; or we may say and do things that harm us or others. Wherever the Holy Spirit leads us, we can trust that He will never lead us to a place of regret.

Raise your hand if you'd like to avoid future regret. Me too!

Scripture warns us not to *grieve* the Holy Spirit through our disobedience, and not to *quench* His Spirit by ignoring His promptings—and as always with good reason. **(Ephesians 4:30; 1 Thessalonians 5:19)**

So, let's fully surrender to the work of the Holy Spirit beginning here and now.

1. Please read **John 14:15-21** to hear Jesus's promise to send the Holy Spirit. How does Jesus describe the Spirit? How does the Holy Spirit unite us to God the Father and Jesus the Son **(John 14:17, 20)**?

2. Turn to **1 Corinthians 6:19-20** and see how we should regard ourselves. How does this encourage you to completely surrender yourself to the Holy Spirit?

Pause now and thank God for His Holy Spirit. Ask Him to help you hear, listen to, and trust His ways, and for a willingness to obey His leading.

Lord, may Your Holy Spirit come, have Your way in me,

Amen.

DAY THREE

Asking for Guidance

Pride often stands in the way of asking for guidance; humility admits our need for help and confesses that we don't know everything or have it all together. Those difficult truths are hard to acknowledge. We like to pretend we are masters at everything, but God knows that's not the case. Shortcomings are nothing to be ashamed of—everyone on this planet has them. God is the only One who is perfect, and He has the master plan. He is familiar with the areas on the map that are obscured from our vision; He is aware of twists and turns in the road up ahead. He sees the hills and valleys, the potholes and puddles. It is wise and good to ask Him for directions. No matter how much we know, He always knows better.

Let's humble ourselves and ask the Master. He knit and wove us together in our mother's womb; every day of our life has already been written in His Book **(Psalm 139:13-18)**. He was present when we took our first steps; He will be with us when we take our last breath; He will be there to welcome us into Heaven someday. The Lord has counted the hairs on our head and recorded our tears on His scroll **(Luke 12:7; Psalm 56:8)**. He is intimately acquainted with the desires of our heart—all the joys and sorrows. God knows our dreams because He placed them there. He gave us our gifts, talents, and skills for a purpose. The condition of our relationships is of no surprise to Him. The job we work at or the ministry in which we serve are all under God's watchful eye. Our Creator knows us better than we know ourselves!

God alone knows which direction we should go, which doors we should walk through, and which ones should stay closed. If it's closed, don't try to pry it open! **Psalm 143:10** is a prayer that we can pray: *"Teach me to do your will, for you are my God; may your good Spirit lead me on level ground."* Seeking God's direction, listening for His voice, and then heeding His call will always lead us on the right course. When He says *wait*, we should pause yet remain attentive. When He says *go*, it's time to lace up our shoes. When He tells us to *stay*, we must look around and ask what He would like to accomplish in that place. Sometimes He leads with a bright glowing fire, other times it's with a billowing cloud. Wherever He leads we can be certain that His protection goes before us, and He is our rear guard **(Isaiah 58:8)**. When following the Lord, He may ask us to leave some things behind—idols, relationships, jobs, comfort, and conveniences. He may take us to places that are outside our comfort zone. Instead of grumbling and complaining, we must trust. God will only lead us to good, abundant spaces. Jesus assures us that whatever we give up for His sake, *we will receive a hundred times as much and will inherit eternal life* in return **(Matthew 19:29)**. That's a generous trade!

1. In **Numbers 9:15-23** we read the story of the Israelites' departure from Egypt. They left the life they knew behind; they followed the Lord to places He had not yet divulged. They trusted God's guidance and knew He was with them every step of the way. Please read these verses and make note of God's faithful guidance.

2. Do you trust God's guidance? How often do you ask Him to show you the way?

Come before the Lord and ask for His guidance. Is there a particular area where you especially need it? Whether it seems unsurmountable or inconsequential, God cares and will guide you in His perfect will—ask Him now.

Lord, please give me guidance,

Amen.

DAY FOUR

Seeking God's Will

There are so many things, people, tasks, responsibilities, roles, and desires that tug on our hearts and cry for our attention. Various viewpoints and voices call for our devotion—political agendas, current social values, the philosophies of this world, the need to fit in and be accepted. These various voices can be beneficial or harmful to our bodies, minds, and spirits. They can complement our faith or steer us totally off course. God warns us not to be taken captive or led astray.

Joshua 1:7-8 shares incredible wisdom for staying true to God's will and ways:

"Be strong and very courageous. Be careful to obey all the law my servant Moses gave you; do not turn from it to the right or to the left, that you may be successful wherever you go. ⁸ Keep this Book of the Law always on your lips; meditate on it day and night, so that you may be careful to do everything written in it. Then you will be prosperous and successful."

The LORD spoke these words to Joshua before leading him across the Jordan river to take possession of enemy territory. Joshua and the Israelites would encounter obstacles and face their adversaries head on. God encouraged them to keep their eyes focused on Him—He was their source of courage and victory. He warned them not to look to the left or right, because doing so might make them discouraged and take them off course. God alone was their hope and salvation; He alone assured their success. Nothing and no one else could save them from their foes. Open your Bible and read **Joshua 1:1-18** for yourself.

The same is true for us. We too will face trials and tribulations. We have an enemy who is seeking to devour us—Satan is his name. The devil would love nothing more than for us to put our hope elsewhere—anywhere other than in our Heavenly Father. His aim is to misguide us. We are warned all throughout Scripture not to look to the left or right to save us, in any given form. We must keep our hearts set on the Lord, fix our minds on His Kingdom. We must seek His will and believe His Word above every other voice that will try to get our attention. The Lord's will and way may look scary or seem impossible—but all things are possible with Him. The Lord can lead us safely across a raging river, by making a way that only He could make—He can miraculously part the waters

(Joshua 3). Seeking the Lord's will is the best place to start any journey. So long as we keep our focus on Him, He will show us the wisest and most desirable way to go. God alone is our secure and eternal hope. He makes us prosper; He goes before us and paves the way. Our victory and security are found in no other Name under Heaven! He brings us into the Promised Land!

Let's not deviate from seeking and following His will alone. Let's turn down the volume and tune out the noise that is continually vying for our attention and allegiance. Let's claim His promises for ourselves and walk in obedience to where He leads us. Let's *be strong and courageous*! Yes, let us!

1. What are some voices that try to get you off track and how do you counteract them?

2. How does, or has, seeking God's will and focusing on Him keep you moving in the right direction? What blessings do you encounter?

Pray now and ask the Lord to help you turn down the static and attune your ears to hear Him more clearly.

O God, help me to hear Your voice,

Amen.

DAY FIVE

Trusting His Plan

We might enthusiastically submit to God's authority. We may long for His Holy Spirit to fill our hearts and guide us in truth. We may earnestly desire to follow the Lord and His ways. We most likely ask, seek, and knock with the intent of responding to God's answers with complete and faithful obedience. But when it really comes down to it, do we wholly trust His methods and timing in every instance. Raise your hand (even though I can't see you) if you are ever tempted to rush ahead of God or take matters into your own hands. Me too! In **Genesis 15, 16, and 17**, we find a Biblical example that warns us against impatience and self-reliance. God had promised Sarai and her husband Abram a son—which would lead to more descendants than there are stars in the sky. And one of those descendants would bless all of humanity by saving us from our sins. You guessed it—I'm talking about Jesus! Well, Sarai and Abram were getting well along in their years, seventy-six and eighty-six to be exact **(Genesis 16:16)**, and Sarai came up with the brilliant scheme to help God along with His plan. She had her husband sleep with and impregnate her maidservant Hagar. Hagar's' story is truly beautiful—I touch on it more in my *"A Daughter of the King"* workbook. But for now, we'll look at this from Sarai's perspective. Because of Sarai's impatience and lack of trust in God's faithfulness to His promises, she made a big mess, not just for herself but for everyone around her. God fulfilled His promise to them when Sarah was 90 and Abraham was 100—they had a son and named him Isaac.

When God says wait, it's for a good reason. Scripture gives us so many wonderful reminders of God's faithfulness. He has never broken a promise or gone back on His Word. We can trust that He is faithful in everything He does, even when it's not according to our timetable or done in the way we'd orchestrate.

> *"For the word of the LORD is right and true; he is faithful in all he does."* Psalm 33:4

We can be confident that God's plans, His purpose for our lives, and His answers to our prayers are always for our good. Knowing this helps us to wait out the process. Answers might arrive in an instant or come after years of pleading on our knees with tear-stained cheeks. Since God sees the big picture, we can trust that He will bring about His perfect plan.

"I remain confident of this: I will see the goodness of the LORD IN the land of the living. ¹⁴ Wait for the LORD; be strong and take heart and wait for the LORD."

Psalm 27:13-14

1. How does Sarai's story inspire you to submit to the Lord's timing and mode of answer in your own life? **(Genesis 15:1-5, 16:1-16; 17:17-21.)**

2. Please read **Psalm 46:1-11.** Reread verse **46:10** specifically. Memorize it and then write it out here:

Now allow your observations and impressions to guide you in prayer. Ask the Lord to help you trust His faithfulness and expertise. Ask Him to help you be still, take heart, and wait on Him.

Dear Sovereign Lord,

Amen.

DAY SIX

Immediate Obedience

When God asks you to do something or nudges you to respond in a certain way, how easily do these words roll off your tongue as they did with Mary in **Luke 1:38**: "*I am the Lord's servant. May your word to me be fulfilled*"? In theory and desire, we are quick to say *yes* and *amen* in agreement, but when push comes to shove and we're presented with a real-life opportunity to obey God, hesitation often comes into play. We want to ponder, question, mull over, and consider the *ifs, when, how, why,* and *what* of the situation before safely proceeding. In essence we want control.

I firmly believe this is because our eyes automatically turn inward, and we reflect on our own inadequacies rather than focus on God's all-sufficiency. We see our weaknesses, we are fully aware of our past failings, and that makes us afraid to let go, trust where the Lord is taking us, and have faith in what He is asking of us. Fixing our eyes *on the Lord*, setting our hearts firmly *on Him*, brings an assurance and confidence in His Almighty plan. If God calls us to do something, he will surely equip us for the task ahead.

Mary, mother of Jesus is our perfect example in this. God asked her to step into the paramount role of her life, and not just hers but the greatest of all mankind. She was a mere teenager when the angel Gabriel paid her a visit and told her that she would give birth to a child—the Son of God. She was a virgin and not yet officially married to her betrothed Joseph, so she asked the angel how this would come about. She took the angel at his word when he said the Holy Spirit would come upon her. Her response was one of immediate obedience. She didn't question her own ability to carry out her role—which was to give birth, care for, and raise the Savior of the world! That's huge! I'm pretty sure God has never and will never call us to such an incredible task. And yet we question, waver, and doubt His plan when it's so small in comparison. Mary is a beautiful example of looking to the Lord and His faithfulness and power—not the impossibility of her situation. She knew God was in charge, and she simply surrendered.

Mary gave her life, her plans, and her future to the Lord as an offering. She knew His character—He is holy, perfect, loving, and just. She chose to believe that He could use even her for His great purpose. Believing God was not something new to Mary. She had trusted the Lord throughout her life, and it was something she would continue to do. She was humble in heart, and that's why she found God's favor—not because she had proven herself worthy through works. She was merely His vessel through which He would bless humanity.

God also desires to use us for His mighty purpose. It might not be as grand as Mary's, but it is essential to His Kingdom. There are people in our lives who will be blessed by our obedience to God's will. And let's not forget the fulfillment that comes to our lives as well.

"Blessed is she who has believed that the Lord would fulfill his promises to her!"

Luke 1:45

1. Join me in reading **Luke 1:26-45** and note your observations.

2. How does Mary's story inspire you to step out in faith and say *yes* to the Lord, without reservation? Imagine what you could be a part of!

Pause and ask the Lord to help you trust His plans, no matter how impossible they seem, and confidently respond with the words, *I am the Lord's servant.*

Dear Lord,

Amen.

DAY SEVEN

Complete Surrender

Submission is expressed through our words and actions. It is felt in our hearts and exhibited through devotion. Our posture, both physical and spiritual, gives great insight and indication as to the surrender of our lives. A posture of awe and reverence is evidenced through our worship to God and the lifting of our praise. A posture of humility and gratitude often causes us to fall to our knees and bow before the Lord.

Ultimate submission means trusting God with our life even to the point of death—in this Jesus is the truest expression. Jesus knew that His crucifixion was imminent and understood the torture that He would soon endure. He knelt in the Garden of Gethsemane praying to His Heavenly Father; tears flowed from His eyes and a mixture of sweat and blood dripped from His brow. He asked *for this cup to pass*, in essence for some other plan to save mankind. Yet in the same instance He prayed *that Father's will be done*, not His own. Jesus knew that following God's plan would bring glory to the Father and salvation to the world **(Luke 22:39-46)**.

> *"Fixing our eyes on Jesus, the pioneer and perfecter of faith. For the joy set before him he endured the cross, scorning its shame, and sat down at the right hand of the throne of God." Hebrews 12:2*

The joy and *the Cross* seem mutually exclusive, but the way Jesus viewed it they clearly went together. The prospect of us being united with Him forever brought Him joy and helped Him endure the Cross. You and I are the joy that Jesus focused on as He carried His Cross and then allowed Himself to be hung on it. Jesus took up His Cross and laid down His life for us. Now He asks us to take up our cross and lay down our lives for the sake of following Him, all the way Home to our Heavenly Father. It is a beautiful exchange!

Jesus exemplified the second line of His prayer: *Your kingdom come, Your will be done on earth as it is in Heaven*. Jesus lived and died for the cause of the Kingdom of Heaven **(see Hebrews 5:7-9)**. He brought the Kingdom to earth with Him and He invites us to enter in. It is our joy and privilege to live for the Kingdom too.

We are exhorted to die to self and live for Christ; to lose our life and genuinely find it. We are commanded to take the Kingdom's Gospel to the ends of the earth starting from right where we are without hesitation **(Matthew 28:16-20)**.

On our own volition this seems overwhelmingly unfeasible, but with the love of God compelling us, the joy of the Lord filling us, and the work of the Holy Spirit empowering us, we can fulfill Jesus' call upon our lives. **Hebrews 12:2** encourages us to *fix our eyes on Jesus, the pioneer [author] and perfector of our faith*. He is the One at work in and through us!

1. Read a little further and find more motivation in **Hebrews 12:3**. How does, or will, this encourage you to completely surrender to the Lord?

2. What does Jesus say about our cross in **Matthew 16:24-28**? Describe the benefits you have experienced as a result of living for the Lord.

Pray for the Lord to give you His perspective and increase your joy in following Him. Ask God to reveal any areas of your life that you need to lay down so that you can pick up your cross today. Thank Him for considering you a *joy*.

Merciful God,

Amen.

"Come, let us sing for joy to the LORD;

let us shout aloud to the Rock of our salvation.

² Let us come before him with thanksgiving

and extol him with music and song.

³ For the LORD is the great God,

the great King above all gods.

⁴ In his hand are the depths of the earth,

and the mountain peaks belong to him.

⁵ The sea is his, for he made it,

and his hands formed the dry land.

⁶ Come, let us bow down in worship,

let us kneel before the LORD our Maker;

⁷ for he is our God

and we are the people of his pasture,

the flock under his care." Psalm 95:1-7

WEEK FOUR

Thanksgiving

"Give thanks in all circumstances...."

Day 1: Entering In

Day 2: Lavish Benefits

Day 3: Every Blessing

Day 4: Joyful Noise

Day 5: Glad Recollections

Day 6: Plentiful Provisions

Day 7: Gracious Gifts

DAY ONE

Entering In

We have a whole week of *Thanksgiving* and even that isn't enough to capture all our gratitude! Prayers of thanksgiving give glory to God, and they are an acknowledgment that all our blessings are gifts from Him. *Every good and perfect gift is from above* **(James 1:17)**. Thanksgiving changes our outlook by opening our eyes to God's perspective. Our *glass half empty* view quickly changes to a *glass half full*. Even when it seems there is nothing to be grateful for, rest assured there is always something worth appreciating, if we just look for it.

We can begin by thanking God for our salvation, for the breath in our lungs and the beating of our heart. The beauty of creation is a great source of inspiration for our words of thanks—from the clouds in the sky, the mountains towering high, and the waves of the ocean rolling in and out; to the trees that sway in the breeze and provide homes for the birds to rest. We can thank the Lord for our health and if our health is currently suffering, we can thank Him for doctors and nurses, and treatments that He uses to ease our ailments. We can thank God for our family and friends that He has placed in our lives. We should thank Him for giving us the Bible which teaches us about Him, and for the amazing privilege of prayer. Thank Him for the eternal hope He offers through Jesus Christ, and the daily hope He brings us through His presence here and now.

As we take time to thank our Father, we are reminded of His goodness to us. Our hearts are revived, and our minds are refocused on truth. Giving thanks lifts our spirits and unburdens our weary souls—hope, courage, peace, and joy take up residence in our lives.

"God gave you the gift of 86,400 seconds today. Have you used one to say thank you?" a quote from William A. Ward.

Gratitude and negativity cannot coexist. The next time your heart feels heavy, or your mind is filled with anxiety, take your thoughts captive and make them obedient to Christ **(2 Corinthians 10:5)**. God will help you see the positive and He will lift you out of the pit. He will set your feet on steady ground and give you a new song to sing **(Psalm 40:2)**.

"Enter his gates with thanksgiving and his courts with praise; give thanks to him and praise his name." Psalm 100:4

1. Please read **Philippians 4:8** and make note of what God's children are supposed to think about. How will this impact your mindset?

2. Read **Psalm 100:1-5** and then list everything you discover about God that motivates your gratitude and praise.

Now comes the time to enter the Lord's gates with thanksgiving and praise. Get your tambourine ready and thank Him for everything that pops into your mind.

Generous Father, I thank you,

Amen.

DAY TWO

Lavish Benefits

The benefits the Lord brings to our lives are abundant, and their ramifications are eternal. Today I'm doing things a little differently—I am going to let God's Word lead us completely. Instead of recounting all His benefits for you, I thought I'd direct you right to the source. After all the Bible says it best!

Please read the following Scriptures to yourself and then read them a second time aloud. Meditate on the words and let them wash over your soul.

"Praise the LORD, my soul; all my inmost being, praise his holy name. ^{2} Praise the LORD, my soul, and forget not all his benefits—^{3} who forgives all your sins and heals all your diseases, ^{4} who redeems your life from the pit and crowns you with love and compassion, ^{5} who satisfies your desires with good things so that your youth is renewed like the eagle's. ^{6} The LORD works righteousness and justice for all the oppressed. ^{7} He made known his ways to Moses, his deeds to the people of Israel: ^{8} The LORD is compassionate and gracious, slow to anger, abounding in love. ^{9} He will not always accuse, nor will he harbor his anger forever; ^{10} he does not treat us as our sins deserve or repay us according to our iniquities. ^{11} For as high as the heavens are above the earth, so great is his love for those who fear him; ^{12} as far as the east is from the west, so far has he removed our transgressions from us. ^{13} As a father has compassion on his children, so the LORD has compassion on those who fear him; ^{14} for he knows how we are formed, he remembers that we are dust." Psalm 103:1-22

This passage exhorts us to remember—and not forget—the immeasurable benefits we have received from the Lord. The rewards described can never be attained by our own effort or earned in our own righteousness. They are gifts of grace that we receive by faith. God removed all possibilities for boasting—He knows us so well. Let's savor the last verse: *"As a father has compassion on his children, so the LORD has compassion on those who fear Him..."* He knows our weaknesses and He steps in to meet our needs. He is loving, gracious, kind, and oh so good to us!

1. Go back and underline every benefit that you have in the Lord. How does recounting God's unmerited favor toward you encourage your heart?

2. Now list and personally receive every benefit you've been given.

Pray now and thank God for every heavenly gift He's lavished upon you.

Praise the Lord, my soul, thank you for the extravagant benefits you have poured out on my life,

Amen.

DAY THREE

Every Blessing

You are a child of God—you are deeply loved; you are completely forgiven; you are made new and washed clean; you are God's beloved and you belong to His family; you matter to the Father; you are His beautiful creation and He made you for a great purpose; you are strong and capable; you are royalty in His heavenly Kingdom. God chose you and me for the purpose of knowing Him. He pours out the best that He has to offer—He offered His own Son to save us and sent His own Holy Spirit to dwell in our hearts. As you read through the following Scripture, please note the references to our *every spiritual blessing in Christ*—they are cited one after another. Underline or highlight the blessings as you go.

"Praise be to the God and Father of our Lord Jesus Christ, who has blessed us in the heavenly realms with every spiritual blessing in Christ. [4] For he chose us in him before the creation of the world to be holy and blameless in his sight. In love [5] he predestined us for adoption to sonship through Jesus Christ, in accordance with his pleasure and will— [6] to the praise of his glorious grace, which he has freely given us in the One he loves. [7] In him we have redemption through his blood, the forgiveness of sins, in accordance with the riches of God's grace [8] that he lavished on us. With all wisdom and understanding, [9] he made known to us the mystery of his will according to his good pleasure, which he purposed in Christ, [10] to be put into effect when the times reach their fulfillment—to bring unity to all things in heaven and on earth under Christ. [11] In him we were also chosen, having been predestined according to the plan of him who works out everything in conformity with the purpose of his will, [12] in order that we, who were the first to put our hope in Christ, might be for the praise of

his glory. ¹³ And you also were included in Christ when you heard the message of truth, the gospel of your salvation. When you believed, you were marked in him with a seal, the promised Holy Spirit, ¹⁴ who is a deposit guaranteeing our inheritance until the redemption of those who are God's possession—to the praise of his glory."
Ephesians 1:3-14

1. God has given us *every* spiritual blessing in the heavenly realms—that means we lack nothing! We are *chosen, adopted, redeemed, forgiven, included, and are sealed with the Holy Spirit as proof*. Which of these words do you most need to hear?

2. How do these truths impact your identity now? And moving forward?

Quiet your heart and thank the Father for making you, His child.

Lord, thank you for loving me and choosing me to be in Your family,

Amen.

DAY FOUR

Joyful Noise

At the beginning of our *Thanksgiving* week, we brought out our tambourines and wrote prayers of gratitude to the Lord. Today let's go a step further and break out the entire band—the harp and lyre, guitar, banjo, bagpipes, cymbals, and drums. I know there's a chance I'm catching you on a less-than-cheery day and you might not feel like giving thanks at the moment, but rejoicing is more than a feeling—it's a choice we must make. And often, once we start counting our blessings, our feelings soon follow suit. **1 Thessalonians 5:18** tells us to, *"give thanks in all circumstances; for this is God's will for you in Christ Jesus."* In case you missed it, the verse says in *all* circumstances! Good days, bad days, sad days, difficult situations, joyful occasions—ALL. This is *God's will* for us in Christ Jesus. Everyone who has placed their faith in Jesus, received salvation, gained eternal life, been blessed with every spiritual blessing, and been adopted into the family of God has reason to be joyful. Our *happiness* is often dependent upon our surroundings—it ebbs and flows based on our environment and emotions. Unshakable, enduring *joy* is based on our relationship with the Lord—it is a deep abiding sense that God is good, and He is in control. The joy of the Lord is steady and constant, and it is our strength in rough seasons **(Nehemiah 8:10)**. It is rooted in faith and built on hope. It is an inner gladness, a sense of delight and rejoicing at all the Lord has done in our lives. We can experience this joy even when we don't feel like smiling. The Greek root definition of *joy* is *an awareness of God's grace and favor; grace recognized* (Biblehub.com). Our worship, praise, gratitude, and thanks are more than words; our joyful noise is an offering to the Lord. Joy has everything to do with being gratefully aware!

"I will praise God's name in song and glorify him with thanksgiving." Psalm 69:30

King David often celebrated with harp, lyre, trumpets, and singing and dancing. He chose to praise and thank God after receiving a great victory. He chose to praise and thank God when he was running for his life and hiding in a cave. Even when his heart was heavy and the weight of the world hung on his mind, he looked to the Lord and praised Him. Focusing on the Lord always turned David's perspective around and lifted his spirit.

Psalm 42:5 records David's words: *"Why, my soul, are you downcast? Why so disturbed within me? Put your hope in God, for I will yet praise him, my Savior and my God."*

This is a great example for us to follow. Whatever the day holds, we can choose to put our hope in the Lord and yet praise Him. We can choose to rejoice in the Lord always **(Philippians 4:4; 1 Thessalonians 5:16)**. We can proclaim, *"this is the day that the Lord has made, I will be glad and rejoice in it!"* **(Psalm 118:24)**.

1. Please read **Psalm 92:1-15** and record everything the psalmist is thankful for. Are you thankful for these things too?

2. Now look up **Psalm 98:1-9** and note the additional reasons we have for rejoicing. How does all the earth join in the celebration?

Come before the Lord with your own words of gratitude. Speak from your heart—ask the Lord to revive your joy and help it overflow.

Lord, I will praise Your Name and glorify You with my thanks,

Amen.

DAY FIVE

Glad Recollections

The entire Bible is a recollection of God's mighty deeds and past faithfulness to His people. The Israelites drew strength and comfort from reflecting on God's goodness to them, and we can do the same. We have the entire Old Testament to inspire us, and we have the New Testament to encourage us too. The Israelites praised the Lord for who He is, and they thanked Him for the blessings in their lives. They thanked God for His goodness, love, protection, deliverance, and salvation. They understood that without His constant presence and help they would have perished in the desert. Every time they approached a new leg in their journey, encountered a fierce enemy, or began a daunting project, they would recall the Lord's mercy, grace, and power. They also confessed their sins and repented of their past behavior. Moses reminded the Israelites of God's blessings over them during their mass exodus from Egypt **(Deuteronomy 11)**. Joshua recounted the nation's history before allowing the people to go and claim their land **(Joshua 24)**. Nehemiah and the Israelites separated themselves from their pagan neighbors and devoted themselves to God. They rehearsed the story of their rebellion, captivity, and redemption, and they renewed their covenant with the Lord **(Nehemiah 9)**. Throughout the book of Acts, we read testimony after testimony of God's endless love and actions among His holy people. The book of **Revelation, chapter 15** gives us a glimpse into Heaven, where we witness eternal praises and thanksgiving being sung in response to the Lord's marvelous deeds.

"I will give thanks to you, LORD, with all my heart; I will tell of all your wonderful deeds." Psalm 9:1

Reflecting on the Lord's past works inspires us to trust Him with our future. We gain assurance for the present, and confidence in bringing our requests to Him. God is the same yesterday, today, and tomorrow. If He was faithful then, He is faithful now. If He was sovereign then, He is sovereign now. If He was loving, kind, good, and merciful then, we can trust that He is all that and more now.

"Give thanks to the LORD, for he is good; his love endures forever." 1 Chronicles 16:34

The people of the Bible leave us many examples—some we should follow and some we should just learn from and avoid. One example we should exemplify is the habit of thanking the Lord for His continual favor and for answered prayers from our past.

1. Please read **Psalm 136** and make note of everything the Israelites had to be thankful for. Notice the repeated phrase which applies to *you* now. How does this comfort you?

2. Surely, God has been with you throughout your life. He has intervened, answered prayers, brought you comfort—possibly overtly or behind the scenes. Maybe you noticed and maybe you are still unaware of these times. Ask God to recall or reveal them to you now. Quiet your heart, still your mind, and listen for His words. What is the Lord recollecting for you?

Consider these memories and bring an offering of thanksgiving to the Lord. Then ask Him to help you move forward with the certainty that He is still working in your life today.

God of Heaven, Your love endures forever,

Amen.

DAY SIX

Plentiful Provisions

Have you ever experienced a personal season of drought? This can refer to a period of emotional, physical, or spiritual dryness. It may also signify a time when financial resources appeared to be evaporating. These phases can be short-lived or seem to stretch on forever. No matter how long they last or how hard they get, God is the one to see us through them. He generously provided for the Israelites as they wandered in the desert for forty long years. The land on which they traversed was dry, barren, and harsh, yet the Lord met their every need. He provided safety, security, shelter, guidance, and favor. When their water supply grew scarce, He brought forth streams from a rock **(Exodus 17; Numbers 20)**. When food was running out, He delivered bread from heaven—referred to as manna—every morning, and fresh quail meat to their camp each night **(Exodus 16)**. God continuously brought plentiful provisions. At first, they were grateful and thanked the Lord for the miracles. As time went on, they grew tired of the same food day after day and became thankless in their hearts. They began to grumble and complain against the Lord God Almighty who had generously sustained them in the desert—and they incurred consequences as a result. The account of the Israelites serves as reminder for us: every good and perfect gift comes from our Father above and He deserves our gratitude.

Exodus 16:31-32 records: *"The people of Israel called the bread manna. It was white like coriander seed and tasted like wafers made with honey. ³² Moses said, "This is what the L*ORD *has commanded: 'Take an omer of manna and keep it for the generations to come, so they can see the bread I gave you to eat in the wilderness when I brought you out of Egypt.'"*

God instructed the Israelites to remember the manna He had provided, and to share their testimony of His goodness with others. Reflecting on how the Lord provided in the past, giving thanks for all He has done, praising Him as generous and good, gives us a joyful, hope-filled perspective for today and the future. We gain the assurance that if He gave us our daily bread yesterday, He will surely supply our daily bread today. God knows exactly what we need and when we need it. He is the source of every good thing, and He is generous and kind.

Next week we will begin bringing our requests to the Lord. Today we are first focusing our minds on thanking God for His past faithfulness to us. Take a moment to reflect on your life and answer these questions for yourself: How has the Lord provided in the past? Are there times when He poured refreshment into your heart? Occasions when He sustained and nourished your soul? Situations where He provided guidance, or seasons when He sheltered you from a storm?

"You answer us with awesome and righteous deeds, God our Savior..." Psalm 65:5

1. Read through the whole passage of **Psalm 65** and record all the ways the Lord meets the needs of His creation. Thank Him for all the ways He has met your needs and supplied your daily bread.

2. Now read **Psalm 23** and note how God met David's needs while he was in a desert place. Have you experienced God's provision in this manner? Explain.

Pray now and thank the Lord for His abundant provisions in the past. Ask Him to help you trust that He will provide for your needs in the days to come.

Dear Lord, my loving Shepherd,

Amen.

DAY SEVEN

Gracious Gifts

I am so grateful that God welcomes me as His child, that He paid for my sins and offers me salvation. The Lord has been so good to me—He has sealed me with His Holy Spirit and promised to come again for me someday. He has lavished me with gift upon gift, and I am eternally grateful. He has blessed you with all the same blessings. He bestows benefits too numerous to count, although on a previous day we did name many of them. In addition to all this, the Lord gives us spiritual gifts so that we are equipped to serve Him and bless others. It is hard enough to fathom that the Lord would desire a relationship with me—it's quite another to consider that He would deem me usable for His Kingdom's work.

The Lord takes all my weaknesses and makes me strong; He mends my heart and fills me with compassion. He seals my brokenness with Holy Spirit glue. I am a weak and empty vessel—that's exactly the kind of person God likes to use! I can do nothing on my own, so He alone gets the glory!

"But we have this treasure in jars of clay to show that this all-surpassing power is from God and not from us." 2 Corinthians 4:7

The Lord gives us spiritual gifts for the express purpose of serving him, for building up His church, and for loving others in His name. We get to be the hands and feet of Jesus—spreading the Good News wherever we go and serving whomever we meet. We season the world with the salt of salvation, with the hope of Heaven, the peace of God, the joy of the Lord, and the righteousness of His Kingdom. We shine God's glorious light in the world, driving back the darkness. What a blessing to serve the Lord in such a manner! **(Matthew 5:13-16)**

"It is God who works in you to will and to act in order to fulfill his good purpose."

Ephesians 2:13

God doesn't need us to be perfect to use us for His purpose; we just have to be willing and available. As we walk in sync with Him, He does all the rest. We go where He leads and do what He asks. It's always a good adventure!

We are His ambassadors—using our God-given talents, skills, resources, and time along with our spiritual gifts to represent His heavenly Kingdom while living on the earth.

The spiritual gifts the Holy Spirit imparts are listed in a few different places in the Bible. Take a peek if you'd like to learn more:

1 Corinthians 12:1-31; Romans 12:3-8; Ephesians 4:11-16

1. Describe your response to the fact that God wants to use you to represent Him? Are you humbled? Awed? Surprised? Honored? Excited? Grateful? Explain.

2. God's all-surpassing power is working in you to do His will. How does this build your confidence?

Now, it's time to pray in response.

Thank you, Lord, for entrusting me with spiritual gifts. I pray to use them for Your glory,

Amen.

"I urge, then, first of all, that petitions, prayers, intercession and thanksgiving be made for all people— ² for kings and all those in authority, that we may live peaceful and quiet lives in all godliness and holiness. ³ This is good, and pleases God our Savior, ⁴ who wants all people to be saved and to come to a knowledge of the truth." 1 Timothy 2:1-4

WEEK FIVE

Requests

"Give us today our daily bread."

Day 1: Assuredly

Day 2: Persistently

Day 3: Earnestly

Day 4: Specifically

Day 5: Boldly

Day 6   Expectantly

Day 7: Faithfully

DAY ONE

Assuredly

We can pray assuredly, knowing that the Lord hears our prayers. We have the confidence of coming before God's throne and being graciously accepted. Jesus is our High Priest interceding for us with the Father. Previously, throughout the Old Testament only the high priest of Israel could access the most holy room in the Temple—the Holy of Holies—once a year. On the Day of Atonement, which is also referred to as Yom Kippur, the priest would enter this most sacred place on earth to offer sacrifices and make atonement for sins on behalf of the nation **(Leviticus 16)**. A breastplate with the names of Israel's twelve patriarchs was worn over his heart. No one else dared enter the sanctuary for fear that their offering would be rejected, and they would be struck dead. A thick curtain separated this area from the outer rooms and a very select few ever saw behind it. The curtain hung in the Temple as a boundary between God's holiness and sinful people—it ensured reverence for the Lord and protection of the people.

This all changed when Jesus went to the Cross on our behalf. His death was the perfect and acceptable sacrifice that eternally paid for our sins. No other sacrifice will ever be needed. At the exact moment of Jesus' death, the Temple curtain was supernaturally torn in two, from top to bottom **(Matthew 27:50-51; Mark 15:38; Luke 23:45)**. We now have access to God's holy presence at any moment and every single day of the year. He will never turn us away. Any time we approach Him, whenever we come to Him in prayer, we will always find that His arms are stretched wide open. He is ready to welcome and receive us, and to pour out His mercy and grace upon us. What a sweet and reassuring blessing!

"Let us then approach God's throne of grace with confidence, so that we may receive

mercy and find grace to help us in our time of need." Hebrews 4:16

We have the assurance of approaching God's throne and we have the assurance that He cares for us. We also have the confidence that He will answer our prayers according to His perfect will for our lives, and for our greatest benefit. When we lay our cares, concerns, worries, and needs before Him, we can always trust His response. We may not see all the details or know the end result, but we have *confidence in what we hope for and assurance about what we do not see.* The answers may not be clear to us, we may not understand the *how* or *why*, but we do know the One in whom we trust and rely.

> *"Now faith is confidence in what we hope for and assurance about what we do not see."* Hebrews 11:1

1. Read **Hebrews 10:22** for more assurance of your standing before the Lord. How does this encourage you to bring your requests to Him daily?

2. Now read **Psalm 71:5-8** and apply these verses to yourself. How has the Lord shown Himself worthy of your confidence?

Pause now, breathe deeply, and ask the Lord to meet your needs with His daily bread of mercy and grace.

Dear Lord, I approach Your throne with the assurance that You hear, see, and care about me,

Amen.

DAY TWO

Persistently

Ask. Seek. Knock. These three simple words depict God's desire for our prayer life. They represent a continual conversation and a persistent presentation of our requests to the Lord. They are not intended to be something we offer once, and then check off our list and move on from. Our prayers are not a bother to God, in fact they are received as a pleasing aroma before His throne. He desires and invites us to come to Him often. When something is heavy on our hearts or weighing on our minds, we can confidently bring it to the Lord. He never grows weary of hearing from us. Asking, seeking, and knocking are ongoing actions that are essential to our spiritual well-being. The Lord says to *ask, and it will be given, to seek and we will find, to knock and the door will be opened* **(Luke 11:5-13)**. Sometimes we immediately receive what we're asking for, but there may also be a waiting period. This doesn't mean God isn't listening and already acting behind the scenes—He assuredly is. Whenever we seek the Lord, we will immediately find Him waiting for us. His comfort, love, hope, peace, and joy are just on the other side of our seeking as well. There are times though, when we desire His wisdom for a situation, His guidance for a decision, His healing for our bodies, His restoration in our relationships and His answers appear delayed. Even when we don't get our resolution right away, we can still trust that God is working in our circumstance, and He will give us what we need. When we knock on the door, we are promised that Jesus is prepared to embrace us on the other side. When we knock on the various doors presented in our life, the Lord will give us knowledge of His will moving forward and He will act on our behalf when we request it. Don't give up on God; He never gives up on you. Just keep asking, seeking, and knocking!

We wouldn't go to the market one time, fill up our basket, and expect to be sustained for our lifetime—we continue to go back often. We don't join a gym, workout once, and expect to build muscle, strength, energy, and endurance—we must frequently put in effort to notice a difference. The same is true of our prayer life—we must come to the Lord often for lasting benefits. He wants us to persist in coming to Him. If it's a prayer that's worth presenting once, it's most likely a prayer worth persistently pursuing.

"Praise be to God, who has not rejected my prayer or withheld his love from me!"

Psalm 66:20

There may be concerns you prayed for long ago and haven't yet seen an answer. Rest assured; the Lord has not forgotten you. He is working on your behalf even when you aren't fully aware of it. I encourage you to continue praying for that miracle of healing, the miracle of restoration in a relationship, the miracle of a loved one accepting Jesus as their Savior, the miracle of a prodigal child returning to God. Allow the word *persistently* to define your prayer life from here on out.

1. Hear the Lord's encouragement for yourself by turning to **Luke 11:5-13** in your Bible. Read **Matthew 7:11** as well. How does God respond to our prayers? What kind of gifts does He give in response to our asking, seeking, and knocking?

2. What have you prayed for in the past that you need to continue praying for now?

Ask, seek, and knock. The Lord is listening.

Dear Heavenly Father,

Amen.

DAY THREE

Earnestly

To really emphasize this message, I'd like to share a handful of synonyms for the word *earnestly* that I came across: *fervently, intently, passionately, intensely, sincerely, genuinely, whole-heartedly, honestly, urgently, soberly*. Would you use these words to describe your prayers? Do they characterize the way you approach God when something is burdening your soul? Do you come to the Lord and lay it all on the table, unreserved? He sees our pain, feels our hurts, hears our cries, and wants to meet our needs. Although the Lord already knows every detail, He wants us to openly share our hearts and concerns with Him. In doing so, we unburden ourselves. God has much bigger shoulders to carry the weight of our worries, and the power to do something about them.

In **Matthew 11:28-29**, Jesus says, *"Come to me, all you who are weary and burdened, and I will give you rest. ²⁹ Take my yoke upon you and learn from me, for I am gentle and humble in heart, and you will find rest for your souls."*

Jesus offers us a beautiful exchange, if only we'd except it—our weariness and burdens traded for His rest. How can we refuse? This exchange is only made possible by relinquishing control and surrendering to His loving authority. Cares and concerns can quickly snowball into all-consuming worries, fears, depression, and anxiety unless we hand them over to the Lord quickly. Praying earnestly means pleading and crying out for Him to move in supernatural ways when it seems all hope is lost. God will do what only He can do! God does the impossible!

Jesus prayed fervently before He went to the Cross of Calvary. He wept and sweat blood as He earnestly prayed to His Father. He poured out His heart and emptied Himself completely. As a result, the Father sent an angel to refresh Jesus and strengthen Him for His difficult road ahead.

"During the days of Jesus' life on earth, he offered up prayers and petitions with fervent cries and tears to the one who could save him from death, and he was heard because of his reverent submission." Hebrews 5:7

The mood of our conversations with the Lord will vary. Sometimes we'll come light-hearted, excitedly rejoicing. Other times, we'll be overwhelmed or downhearted and want to share our pain. Our interactions may be marked by smiles and laughter, or with tears streaming down our face. We can approach the Lord passionately, fervently, intensely, and urgently—He understands and deeply empathizes **(Hebrews 4:15)**. There may be moments when our earnest prayers are so intense that we're left grasping for words. This is when God's Spirit intercedes on our behalf. It's not the length of our prayer that matters, but our sincerity.

"In the same way, the Spirit helps us in our weakness. We do not know what we ought to pray for, but the Spirit himself intercedes for us through wordless groans."

Romans 8:26

1. Please read **Luke 22:39-44** to witness Jesus earnestly pray to His Father. How are you assured that Jesus empathizes with your suffering?

2. What is weighing on your heart that you need to earnestly pray about?

Beseech the Lord, lay down your cares, and receive His rest.

O Lord, You understand; please help me in my weakness,

Amen.

DAY FOUR

Specifically

Matthew 20:29-34 shares the story of a miraculous healing and a pivotal question: *"As Jesus and his disciples were leaving Jericho, a large crowd followed him. ³⁰ Two blind men were sitting by the roadside, and when they heard that Jesus was going by, they shouted, 'Lord, Son of David, have mercy on us!' ³¹ The crowd rebuked them and told them to be quiet, but they shouted all the louder, 'Lord, Son of David, have mercy on us!' ³² Jesus stopped and called them. <u>'What do you want me to do for you?'</u> he asked. ³³ 'Lord,' they answered, 'we want our sight.' ³⁴ Jesus had compassion on them and touched their eyes. Immediately they received their sight and followed him.*

The men in our story were desperate for the healing touch of Jesus. They cried out for Him to show mercy on them. Their need was obvious to Jesus, but He made them acknowledge it aloud. Jesus posed a very poignant question to the men beside the road—*what do you want me to do for you?* They wanted their sight, but He gave them so much more. He renewed their lives, their hope, their identity, their place of belonging within society, the ability to work and the possibility to earn a living. He restored their dignity. The men could have given a variety of answers, but they gave a specific reply to Jesus' question—they wanted their vision restored. As the men cried out and others tried to shush them, Jesus stopped and had compassion on them. He paused and listened; He cared and acted accordingly. Jesus reached out and personally touched them, bringing them sight—He intimately responded to their needs and brought immediate healing.

Jesus poses the same question to *you* today, and tomorrow, and the day after. What do *you* want Jesus to do for you? Do you need hope and comfort today? Wisdom and a knowledge of God's will for your situation? Strength for your journey ahead? Healing for your body? Or do you also want your vision restored so that you can see with the Lord's perfect perspective? Our answers can be considered as requests for *daily bread*. We know and trust that like the blind men, the Lord will have compassion on us and meet our needs too. We are invited to pray with specific requests. We don't have to beat around the bush with Jesus. We can pray for our exact needs and for the necessities of others—interceding on their behalf, with explicit appeals too.

God is good and He is never too busy for us! He will meet us on the road, alone in the quiet, or in the crowd amid the noise. He will pause, touch, speak, listen, empathize, heal, and give direction. He invites and calls us to follow Him; His love and compassion compels us to leave everything behind to do so.

1. Read **Isaiah 42:5-7** and observe what the Scriptures say regarding our eyes. Who gives us sight and why?

"Open my eyes that I may see wonderful things in your law." Psalm 119:1

2. How has the Lord opened your eyes—through His love, His Word, His promises? To His hope, His peace, His joy, His security? **(Psalm 19:8.)**

Thank the Lord for opening your eyes and giving you a revelation of Him, His love, and His hope **(Ephesians 1:18)**. Then ask Him to meet your specific needs right now. He is asking; now is your chance to reply.

Dear Lord,

Amen.

DAY FIVE

Boldly

The Hebrew word for *bold* is based on *confidence, trust, security,* and *reliance* (Biblehub.com). We can be bold because our confidence is based in the Lord and our trust is founded on His enduring faithfulness. He is our source of security and is the One on whom we can always rely! Our faith in God instills boldness in us. Based on Jesus' perfect sacrifice, we approach His throne with confidence, knowing we will not be turned away. **Proverbs 28:1** describes God's followers in this way: *"the righteous are as bold as a lion."* Our boldness is not rooted in self-reliance, but our reliance on the One who hears and receives our prayers.

Joshua 10:12-14 tells the story of God's faithful and righteous leader, Joshua, and the audacious prayer he prayed. The Israelites were embroiled in battle and needed more hours in the day to ensure their victory. We often ask the Lord to multiply our time and efforts for accomplishing His purpose and the tasks that fill our calendar— and the Lord graciously complies. But in the account of Joshua, we see that he boldly prays for the sun to stand still, and it literally and miraculously does! (Read this passage and see for yourself!) This is the one and only time that God stopped the sun and held the moon in its place. It happened because Joshua was bold enough to ask.

In the New Testament we read about the countless miracles Jesus performed; there were healings of every kind **(Matthew 4:23)**, and the feeding of thousands of men, women, and children with a few fish and loaves **(Matthew 14 and 15)**. There's an account of Jesus casting a legion of demons out of a man and restoring him to his right mind **(Luke 8:26-39)**. Jesus built trust and He gained people's confidence. Word quickly spread among the region about the Messiah and the power that He held.

Three of the Gospels give us the testimony of a woman who boldly approached Jesus with the hope of being healed. Her story is found in **Matthew 9:20-22, Mark 5:21-34,** and **Luke 8:40-48**. The woman had been bleeding for twelve long years with no reprieve from her ailment. She had sought the expertise of doctor after doctor, but her symptoms persisted. Her condition would have rendered her ritually unclean under Jewish Law and excluded her from society. She was undoubtedly disheartened and weak, and most likely anemic. When she saw

Jesus, she saw hope. She forced her way through the masses and boldly reached out to grasp the hem of His garment. Jesus turned to the crowd and asked who touched Him—although He knew perfectly well it was her. Trembling with fear, she spoke up—she bravely told her story and boldly confessed her belief in His power to help her. Her resolute faith invited the Lord's power to move in her life as she expected. Jesus healed her instantly—her bleeding immediately stopped. In response to the woman's fearless conviction, Jesus told her to *"go in peace and be freed from your suffering."*

1. Read the woman's story in **Mark 5:21-34**. How does she inspire you to be bold in your faith and in approaching the Lord with your requests?

2. What do you need to reach out and touch Jesus' hem for today? For what do you need restoration, redemption, or healing?

Drawing from the examples of Joshua and the woman, write a prayer boldly asking the Lord to do what only He can do in your life, or in the lives of your loved ones. He has the authority to stop time; He has the power stop the bleeding. Bring your audacious prayers to Him now and believe that He will answer.

Lord, You alone are my hope. You are the God of miracles,

Amen.

DAY SIX

Expectantly

Do you believe that God hears your prayers? Do you know without a doubt that He cares? When you pray do you expect God to answer? One of the most wonderful gifts that a child of God has, is the confident knowledge that God does indeed hear, care, and act in response to our prayers. There is a huge difference between wishes and prayers—wishes are unfounded hopes and dreams of something we'd like to happen but aren't quite sure they will. Wishes float aimlessly, without anywhere solid to land. Prayers on the other hand, rise directly from our lips to the Throne Room of God—our prayers land firmly in God's capable hands. They are a pleasing offering that He gladly receives **(Acts 10:4)**.

Our prayers of expectancy well up from our knowledge of God's character—He is Creator and Sustainer; He is holy, sovereign, all-powerful, loving, and kind. We know and trust that He answers our prayers when they are in accord with His perfect will. We know His perfect will by reading His Word. The Bible gives us many examples of people who prayed expectantly based on their knowledge of the Lord.

The book of **1 Kings, chapters 17 and 18** details the doubtless prayers of a man named Elijah, and how God met his expectancy with action. **1 Kings 17:17-24** captures the extremes of Elijah's confident petitions—his prayers brought a widow's only son back to life. In **1 Kings 18** we see Elijah come against the false prophets of the pagan gods, Baal and Asherah on top of Mount Carmel. He declared a holy battle to turn the nation of Israel back to the One True God. They had been led astray to worship other gods and idols alongside the God of Israel; this was an abomination in the eyes of the Lord, and it greatly distressed Elijah. The challenge was to set up altars and whichever god consumed the sacrifice by fire was proven worthy of all praise and devotion. The false prophets raved all day long—frantically praying, dancing, cutting themselves until blood flowed, all in an effort to get their gods attention—to no avail. Elijah even mocked them. When the time came for him to call upon the Lord, he did so calmly, briefly, confidently, and expectantly, and God responded with an all-consuming fire from Heaven **(1 Kings 18:36-39)**. Immediately following this expectant prayer and magnificent display of God's power, Elijah fell to the ground and began praying for rain to return to the land—he had previously proclaimed a three-and-a-half-year drought for their rebellion. He was so expectant that he kept sending his servant to look out over the sea for any developing clouds. Time after time the servant came back and reported clear skies—seven times to be exact. Elijah continued praying and soon the servant proclaimed that a cloud the size of a man's fist was rising from the sea **(1 Kings 18:44)**. Elijah prayed expectantly in all these circumstances, and God heard his prayers.

1. Before you start thinking this can't happen for you, I'd like you to read **James 5:16-18**. How is Elijah described? How does this encourage you?

2. Resurrection of life to your weary body or soul, undeniable miracles from above, rain from heaven to refresh your heart—what impossible thing do you need to start praying expectantly for?

"The prayer of a righteous person is powerful and effective." James 5:16

Take your answers from the previous questions and offer them to the Lord now. Pray boldly, pray confidently, pray peacefully, pray expectantly.

LORD, the God of Abraham, Isaac, and Israel, let it be known today that you are God (1 Kings 18:36),

Amen.

DAY SEVEN

Faithfully

Jesus led by example—He prayed often and alone, and at gatherings with others. He gave thanks when breaking bread. Communion with His Heavenly Father brought Him wisdom, power, and strength. He taught us to pray using The Lord's Prayer as our guide. Each line in the benediction represents another heartfelt topic we can bring to the Lord. Jesus understood the significance of prayer, and He taught regarding the practice in other instances too.

In **Matthew 21:13** Jesus said, *"My house will be called a house of prayer."* Out of all the good things He could have called it, He proclaimed His house is a house of prayer! It is a house where God is Father; it is a home where love and acceptance abound. It is a place of safety and security. It is a refuge from the storms of this world. God's house is where we draw near and talk to Him through prayer. God's house is amazing and it's where we are invited to dwell.

We receive salvation by faith in the grace of God, through Jesus Christ, the Son. Our relationship with God begins with a confession of faith. Our prayers to the Lord are spoken in hopeful faith that He hears us. By faith we pray in Jesus' Name knowing that He alone is *the way, the truth, and the life*, and our access to the Father **(John 14:6)**. Faith is the key to every blessing that is ours in the heavenly realms. Jesus spoke a lot about faith and the integral part it plays in our prayers.

Matthew 21:21-22 shares this exhortation: *"Jesus replied, '"Truly I tell you, if you have faith and do not doubt, not only can you do what was done to the fig tree, but also you can say to this mountain, 'Go, throw yourself into the sea,' and it will be done. ²² If you believe, you will receive whatever you ask for in prayer.'"*

In **Luke 17:5-6**, *"The apostles said to the Lord, 'Increase our faith!' ⁶ He replied, 'If you have faith as small as a mustard seed, you can say to this mulberry tree, "Be uprooted and planted in the sea," and it will obey you.'"*

Matthew 17:20 assures us that we can not only uproot the obstacles in our path, we can also move mountains that loom in our way. *"Truly I tell you, if you have faith as small as a mustard seed, you can say to this mountain, 'Move from here to there,' and it will move. Nothing will be impossible for you."*

There is no question that faith is essential! Keep in mind though, that it's not the size of our faith that matters; it's *who* our faith is in. We ask, seek, and knock because we have faith. With faith, we hope and expect the Lord to answer... at least most of the time. To be honest, there are moments when our faith wavers and our confidence wanes. We want to believe with all our heart, but a little doubt lingers and gets in the way of our full surrender. Take heart, there is a story about this exact struggle in the Bible. A man asks Jesus to heal his ailing son, and Jesus first confronts him with his doubt. The man desperately cries out in faith to the One who can help him, *"I do believe; help me overcome my unbelief!"* **(Mark 9:24)**. Jesus didn't rebuke the man for his hesitation but had mercy on him.

1. I'd like you to read the story of this man's plea for greater faith and how Jesus met him. You can find it in **Mark 9:14-29**. Write out **verses 23-24**.

2. What metaphorical *mulberry trees* or *mountains* do you need moving?

Let's pray. Ask God to meet your unbelief with an assurance that He will satisfy your needs, and you can *do all things through Christ who strengthens you* **(Philippians 4:13)**!

Lord, I do believe. Help me overcome any reservation,

Amen.

"Come and hear, all you who fear God;

let me tell you what he has done for me.

[17] I cried out to him with my mouth;

his praise was on my tongue.

[18] If I had cherished sin in my heart,

the Lord would not have listened;

[19] but God has surely listened

and has heard my prayer.

[20] Praise be to God,

who has not rejected my prayer

or withheld his love from me!" Psalm 66:16-20

WEEK SIX

Confession

"And forgive us our debts, as we also have forgiven our debtors."

Day 1: In the Open

Day 2: Search My Heart

Day 3: Removing Barriers

Day 4: Dead to Sin

Day 5: Forgiving Like God

Day 6   Repentance and Revival

Day 7: A Fresh Start

DAY ONE

In the Open

Our first and most important confession is one of faith—**Romans 10:9** tells us: *"If you declare with your mouth, 'Jesus is Lord,' and believe in your heart that God raised him from the dead, you will be saved."* This confession of faith is truly life changing for us, both presently and eternally. After declaring our belief in Jesus as Savior we must also rightly align our lives with Him as Lord. This requires acknowledging our sins and surrendering our body, mind, and spirit to Him. He is aware of every one of our intentional sins and each subconscious transgression, and He loves us nonetheless. Every detail of our lives is laid bare before Jesus—He sees the surface layer and deep within our hearts—and He wants to address it all. He sets out to meet us with the purpose of drawing us into a relationship with Himself and bringing everything out into the open. He knows that's where our healing begins.

"Whoever conceals their sins does not prosper, but the one who confesses and renounces them finds mercy." Proverbs 28:13

John 4:1-42 shares the story of Jesus' encounter with a Samaritan woman—also known as *the woman at the well*. She is referred to in this way because her life-altering conversation with Jesus occurred at a well beside the road. Theirs was not a chance encounter—Jesus purposefully went to this specific town, at this exact time of day, to meet this special woman. She was well known by the townspeople as an outcast woman with a scandalous lifestyle. She avoided their interaction because she knew it meant rejection, gossip, shame, and pain. Other women went to draw their water from the well early in the morning or in the cool of the late afternoon, while she went under the sweltering midday sun. Jesus arrived and sat down at the well precisely as she showed up. A conversation ensued, and Jesus went straight to the matter of her heart. He brought into the open everything she had desperately wanted to forget and hide. Jesus noted that she had been married five times and was currently living with her boyfriend. He didn't bring up her past or current situation to shame her, but to free her from its grip. Jesus was aware of every detail and yet He lovingly pursued a relationship with her. This realization drastically changed her life for the better—she knew she was unconditionally loved and accepted. Her shame was instantly gone, her disgrace was removed, her freedom was gained that day. She had been searching for love and acceptance for so many years; her soul was thirsty, and she hadn't even realized it until Jesus brought it to her attention. Her jar would continue to run dry, but Jesus offered her Living Water so she would never thirst again. He would satisfy her every desire and fulfill every longing of her heart; He would make her whole. Because of the change that occurred inside of her, she became a living testimony of the love, mercy, grace, and acceptance of Christ to others.

The Lord asks us to confess our sins so that we can receive His mercy too. He invites us to unburden ourselves of the shame and regret that imprison and isolate us; He loves us unconditionally and wants us to step out of the darkness and walk in the light with Him. His Living Water cleanses and refreshes our spirits.

1. Read **John 4:1-42** and record Jesus' love and compassion towards the woman. Write out verses **4:10** and **4:14**.

2. Is there something you have been too ashamed to confess to the Lord for fear that he will reject you? Explain.

I encourage you to bring it into the open now. The Lord will meet you with love, mercy, forgiveness, and freedom. Pray now and receive His Living Water.

Lord, forgive me of my sins and fill me with springs of Living Water,

Amen.

DAY TWO

Search My Heart

God's ways are higher than our ways **(Isaiah 55:8-9)**; His holiness is beyond our comprehension **(Revelation 4:8)**. He is consummately perfect in every possible way. He is pure to His core; there is no flaw in Him. We on the other hand, are marred with the smudges from sins that have left their mark. We are tainted with impurities that the Lord wants to cleanse. He desires to make us holy; set apart for Him and His great purpose. He refines us like precious metals of silver and gold until His reflection shines in our lives **(Psalm 66:10)**.

Coming into a relationship with Jesus brings us face-to-face with the reality of our fallen condition and this makes us mourn our sinful choices **(Matthew 5:40)**. Our remorse leads us to repentance—we turn from our sins to follow the Lord in the opposite direction—and there we find grace in abundance **(2 Corinthians 7:10)**. As we begin to clear out the clutter of our sins, some we're not even aware of may stay hidden and linger behind. That's why it's so important that in addition to praying for forgiveness, we also pray for the Lord to search our hearts and bring to our attention anything else we may need to deal with. The Lord knows us better than we know ourselves. He knows our thoughts; He is aware of our motives even when we don't fully understand them ourselves. Sin begins in our *hearts* and overflows through our attitudes, words, and actions—so that is where the Lord begins His purification process **(Matthew 15:18-19; Mark 7:20-23)**.

"You have searched me, LORD, and you know me. ² You know when I sit and when I rise; you perceive my thoughts from afar. ³ You discern my going out and my lying down; you are familiar with all my ways. ⁴ Before a word is on my tongue you, LORD, know it completely." Psalm 139:1-4

"Search me, O God, and know my heart; test me and know my anxious thoughts. ²⁴ Point out anything in me that offends you, and lead me along the path of everlasting life." Psalm 139:23-24 NLT

God's good purpose is to remake us more and more into the likeness of His Son, a little more each day and through every circumstance **(Romans 8:28-29)**. This means that we let go of certain things while grabbing hold of others. Everything we give up for the Lord's sake pales in comparison to blessings He gives in return. Cleansing our lives of sin begins with us first recognizing them.

1. Read **Psalm 139:1-12** and note how deeply familiar the Lord is with you.

2. Now read **Psalm 139:13-18** and share the emotions that wash over you regarding God's involvement in your life and His loving care.

Pray to the Lord who knows you and loves you. Ask Him to search your heart and bring to mind anything you need to confess and surrender. Ask Him to lead you along His path of everlasting life—it's full of blessings!

Search me, O God,

Amen.

DAY THREE

Removing Barriers

Sin holds our hearts hostage and erects a barrier between us and God. Sin steals our joy and saps our strength. It covers us with shame and fills us with regret. It obscures our vision of the Lord; it clogs our ears so that we cannot hear Him clearly. It hardens our hearts, so we are no longer receptive to His leading. Sin is deceptive and makes enticing promises that it cannot deliver. Sin is something the Lord wants to help us deal with. God wants to free our hearts and tear down the walls that stand in the way of our relationship with Him. He offers to restore our joy and renew our strength so that we soar like eagles on the currents above **(Isaiah 40:31)**. He forgives our sins and wraps us in Jesus' righteousness. He faithfully replaces our regret with the hope that His mercies are new each morning **(Lamentations 3:23)**. We need only confess our iniquities to Him. Baring our souls to the Lord can seem scary, but we can rest assured, He will always meet our confessions with tender and gracious mercy. He is so good, loving, and kind. He desires that all barriers of sin be destroyed, so that we can come to Him unhindered. He only wants the best for us and that requires acknowledging our transgressions **(Psalm 32:1-5)**.

It is good for us to be troubled by our sin; it means God is at work and doing a new thing in us. Clearing the clutter from our hearts and minds will help us to see God better. Sin is dark, gloomy, and messy. Confession brings light, clarity, and order to our lives. I'm sure we all want to claim and experience that for ourselves!

"For day and night your hand was heavy on me; my strength was sapped as in the heat of summer. ⁵ Then I acknowledged my sin to you and did not cover up my iniquity. I said, 'I will confess my transgressions to the LORD.*' And you forgave the guilt of my sin."* Psalm 32:4-5

"I confess my iniquity; I am troubled by my sin." Psalm 38:18

"Blessed are the pure in heart, for they will see God." Matthew 5:8

The authors of the Bible were authentic in their writings. They were raw and vulnerable in admitting their shortcomings. We can learn a lot from them. They share with us the key to an unhindered relationship with the Lord, which is ongoing confession. Accepting Jesus as Lord and Savior covers our sins—past, present, and future. Confessing our sins as they continue to occur keeps them from entangling us and prevents them from coming between us and our loving Father **(Hebrews 12:1)**.

1. **Psalm 51** was written by King David after committing egregious sins. Please read **Psalm 51:1-19** and make note of David's confessions, and what he asks of the Lord.

2. How does David's prayer inspire you to confess your sins as they arise?

I love borrowing prayers from Scripture and making them my own. You can use **Psalm 51** to guide your prayer of confession. You can pray it word for word or personalize it to fit your current circumstances.

Have mercy on me, O God,

Amen.

DAY FOUR

Dead to Sin

Repentance is a twofold action. It requires leaving our sin behind and pursuing Christ instead. We were released from the shackles of sin for the purpose of walking in righteousness from the moment we gave our lives to the Lord. We are called to continually abide in Jesus—and then to think, act, speak, live, and breathe in response to all that He pours into our lives. We cannot attain righteousness on our own, and we cannot maintain it by self-effort. We need Jesus every step of the way. He saved us for the purpose of bringing us new life. Jesus bore our sin on the Cross and died in our place. He also rose from the grave victorious over death. The tomb is empty! He is alive and we are made alive in Christ. First, we must die to our old sinful self—it no longer has a place in our lives. We are then free to run with Him in complete abandon.

"In the same way, count yourselves dead to sin but alive to God in Christ Jesus."

Romans 6:11

In **Colossians 3:1-17** Paul strongly exhorts us, *"Put to death, therefore, whatever belongs to your earthly nature: sexual immorality, impurity, lust, evil desires and greed, which is idolatry."* These passages also give us a clear picture of our new life in Christ: *"Therefore, as God's chosen people, holy and dearly loved, clothe yourselves with compassion, kindness, humility, gentleness and patience."*

Clearly our sinful nature and a spirit-filled life are in direct conflict with each other. That's why one must die for the other to live. Baptism is a beautiful picture of this transaction. Although we are saved the moment we invite Jesus into our hearts, baptism is an outward expression of the faith that has come to dwell in us. During baptisms at our church, the person onstage steps into the water, and as they lean back and are fully submerged, the congregation pronounces the follower of Jesus, *"dead to sin."* As they emerge from the water, we all proclaim their victory over death and their newness of life with the words, *"Alive in Christ!"* During the summer months these baptisms take place at the beach where the waves demonstrate God's power to wash away our sins. We are made alive for the purpose of walking with our Lord.

"Therefore, if anyone is in Christ, the new creation has come: The old has gone,

the new is here!" 2 Corinthians 5:17

There may be things coming to mind that you know are against God's will for you. There may be others that you do not consider sins at all. We usually equate sin with big things like murder, stealing, and adultery; but gossip, jealousy, discord, and slander are sins as well. God wants us to die to all these things—they stand in opposition with His will for our lives. They have no part in living for Christ.

1. Please read **Romans 6:11-14** and consider, are you *"offering every part of yourself to him as an instrument of righteousness?"* Is there an area you have been withholding? Elaborate.

2. Now read **Galatians 5:13-26** and consider, are you *"living by the Spirit and keeping in step with Him?"* Do you notice new fruit in your life?

Take your considerations and bring them to the Lord. Present yourself as an offering and ask Him to help you bear fruit in keeping with your new life in Christ.

Dear God, I am so grateful for all You have done. Help me to live for you.

Amen.

DAY FIVE

Forgiving Like God

God desires that we experience His peace, but that is only possible when we release our hatred, bitterness, and unforgiveness to His loving care and sovereign judgment. I'm sure you have noticed that ruminating on your hurts, pain, and resentment only intensifies these emotions. Focusing on the past and on your enemy allows them continued control over your life here and now, keeping you hostage. Every second they are given free rein in your mind is time lost and blessings stolen. God wants to set you free so that you can live in the moment with Him. I understand, and God knows the betrayal you may have faced and the suffering you may have endured at the hands of another—it is very significant because you truly matter.

God commands us to forgive others as He has forgiven us—completely, forever **(Matthew 6:13-14)**. This is not an easy standard to live up to, but with the Holy Spirit's help it is achievable. The Holy Spirit can change our hearts in unconceivable ways, turning our hatred into pity and even compassion. Jesus tells us to bless and pray for our enemies—it may serve as a consolation to know that Jesus also said it is like heaping burning coals of conviction on their heads **(Matthew 5:44; Romans 12:20)**. I know that's a hard pill to swallow, but praying for them releases our hearts and proves our faith in God's justice. He does not turn a blind eye to our suffering or injustice—He is our defender and holy judge. He deals with all sin, He holds everyone accountable for their actions—both good and bad, and He brings about consequences in response **(2 Corinthians 5:10)**. Releasing our unforgiveness to the Father does not let the other person off the hook; God will deal with them accordingly on our behalf. Our natural response to betrayal in any form is that of bitterness, rage, slandering their name, and having malice in our hearts. God wants us to remember the forgiveness He showed us while we were His enemies and extend that same forgiveness in His Name.

"Get rid of all bitterness, rage and anger, brawling and slander, along with every form of malice. ³² Be kind and compassionate to one another, forgiving each other, just as in Christ God forgave you." Ephesians 4:31-32

Forgiveness is for our own good. If not dealt with immediately, bitter roots grow quickly and entangle us completely. They suffocate us and steal the joy the Lord intends for us to have. Bitter roots in our hearts cause trouble for us and are not a good testimony to others. That's why they must be uprooted and laid at the foot of the Cross where the Lord will take care of it. Forgiveness is something we must stick with—the devil will continue to bring things to mind and attempt to plant seeds of bitterness. We must continually pull them out before they grow.

"Make every effort to live in peace with everyone and to be holy; without holiness no one will see the Lord. ¹⁵ See to it that no one falls short of the grace of God and that no bitter root grows up to cause trouble and defile many." Hebrews 12:14-15

1. Read **Romans 5:10** and note the extent of God's forgiveness towards you.

2. Paul, an ambassador of Christ, gave us encouragement on forgiveness in **2 Corinthians 2:9-11.** Are you aware of Satan's schemes to entangle you with bitterness? Are you being obedient in forgiveness? Explain.

Pray and ask the Lord to give you supernatural faith and strength to forgive your debtors just as He has forgiven your trespasses. Ask Him to wash you in His peace and bring justice on your behalf.

Dear Merciful Lord,

Amen.

DAY SIX

Repentance and Revival

In **Daniel 9:3-11** we hear Daniel's prayer of repentance, both for himself and God's people: *"So I turned to the Lord God and pleaded with him in prayer and petition, in fasting, and in sackcloth and ashes. ⁴ I prayed to the LORD my God and confessed: 'Lord, the great and awesome God, who keeps his covenant of love with those who love him and keep his commandments, ⁵ we have sinned and done wrong. We have been wicked and have rebelled; we have turned away from your commands and laws. ⁶ We have not listened to your servants the prophets, who spoke in your name to our kings, our princes and our ancestors, and to all the people of the land. ⁷ "Lord, you are righteous, but this day we are covered with shame—the people of Judah and the inhabitants of Jerusalem and all Israel, both near and far, in all the countries where you have scattered us because of our unfaithfulness to you. ⁸ We and our kings, our princes and our ancestors are covered with shame, LORD, because we have sinned against you. ⁹ The Lord our God is merciful and forgiving, even though we have rebelled against him; ¹⁰ we have not obeyed the LORD our God or kept the laws he gave us through his servants the prophets. ¹¹ All Israel has transgressed your law and turned away, refusing to obey you.'"*

We can pray Daniel's prayer for ourselves, our communities, our nation, and our world. What an exceptionally different place our planet would be if we all repented. In **2 Chronicles 7:14** we find God's invitation to His people:

"If my people, who are called by my name, will humble themselves and pray and seek my face and turn from their wicked ways, then I will hear from heaven, and I will forgive their sin and will heal their land."

Deuteronomy 7:5-6 gives instruction to the Israelites on the importance of destroying their idols and turning their hearts back to God: *"This is what you must do. You must break down their pagan altars and shatter their sacred pillars. Cut down their Asherah poles and burn their idols. ⁶ For you are a holy people, who belong to the LORD your God. Of all the people on earth, the LORD your God has* *chosen you to be his own special treasure."* These same instructions apply to us personally, and they apply to all of God's children as well. If we want to see revival in our world it must first begin in *our* hearts and in the life of every Bible-believing, Jesus-loving, God-fearing person in our churches too. Repentance and revival begin with God's children. Fire begins with one spark and grows into a raging blaze when fanned. Righteousness will take over the earth when God's people tear down their idols and begin living passionately for Him. We can't expect those who don't know the Lord, to live as if they do. But those of us who do know Him bear a great responsibility—we are accountable to God, because we are *called by His Name*. We must humble ourselves and pray for repentance and revival like Daniel.

1. Read **Psalm 85:1-13** for a beautiful display of God's mercy upon His people when they return to Him. List the blessings that are mentioned.

2. What comfort or encouragement do these verses bring to you?

Take a moment to pray for revival in your own heart, and then intercede on behalf of God's people and for our world.

Lord God, I plead with You in prayer and petition,

Amen.

DAY SEVEN

A Fresh Start

Our past sins, mistakes, and failures do not define us. God's grace gives us a new identity. We are His beloved children, forgiven and unblemished, washed clean in the blood of the Lamb, clothed in righteousness, enrobed in fine linen of white. The Bible is full of examples of people just like us—people who failed miserably and then experienced the mercy of God. When all hope seems lost and we are haunted with reminders of our past, God steps in to rewrite our story with a much better plot line that ends in our glory.

Peter was one of Jesus' dearest friends and disciples. He devoted his life to following Jesus wherever He led. He proclaimed his faith and declared he would never deny Jesus as Lord. Yet, on the night before Jesus' crucifixion, Peter vehemently denied his friend three times just as Jesus had predicted. Peter was overcome by the depths of his sin, and he wept bitterly as he realized his betrayal **(Matthew 26)**. Fortunately for Peter, and for us, this is not the end of his story. After Jesus' resurrection, He met Peter on the shore of the Sea of Galilee and gave him a chance at complete redemption. Jesus not only forgave and restored His relationship with Peter, but He also entrusted him with sharing the Good News of His resurrection, starting the church, and feeding His sheep **(John 21)**. Peter was given a fresh start that morning. So are we!

Paul was a devout religious Jew who hated Christians and sought to stop and destroy them. He thought their views were a blaspheme of God Almighty. He didn't understand that Jesus was the fulfillment of all Old Testament Law and prophecies. Jesus chose this man who formerly gave approval to the killing of believers and desired to arrest them, to carry His message of salvation to everyone, both Jew and Gentile. Jesus met Paul on the road to Damascus and forever changed his life **(Acts 9)**. Paul was given a fresh start that day. So are we!

Our fresh start brings with it a new purpose—one that is devoted to serving the Lord and proclaiming His Message of Salvation. God is so good; He does not leave us where He finds us. He brings us to open pastures and quiet streams. He calls us to a life of adventure and brand-new spectacular dreams. He has a part for us to play in His Kingdom and that requires our letting go of the past and straining forward to the future—one day at a time with Him as Lord.

Forgiving ourselves plays a big part in our journey forward. The Bible says that God has removed our sins from us as far as the east is from the west—that is a huge distance! If God who is perfectly holy can forgive us our sins and overlook our past, then we should trust Him enough to forgive ourselves too. Regret and shame only hold us back. Peter and Paul could have stayed in a place of guilt and allowed self-condemnation to dictate the rest of their lives, but they didn't. They believed Jesus when He said they were forgiven. So should we!

Praise God, we are a new creation! **2 Corinthians 5:17** bears repeating: *"Therefore, if anyone is in Christ, the new creation has come: The old has gone, the new is here!"*

1. Read **2 Corinthians 5:16-21.** What does God's forgiveness mean for us who are *in Christ*? How does this impact you personally?

2. How does God want to use your redeemed life for His purpose?

Call on the Lord and ask Him to help you forgive yourself for past transgressions. Ask Him to help you believe you are a new creation in Christ, with a fresh purpose for your life.

Dear Lord, You are the author of new life,

Amen.

"Guard my life and rescue me;

do not let me be put to shame,

for I take refuge in you.

²¹ May integrity and uprightness protect me,

because my hope, LORD, is in you.

²² Deliver Israel, O God,

from all their troubles!" Psalm 25:20-22

WEEK SEVEN

Protection

"And lead us not into temptation, but deliver us from the evil one."

Day 1: Draw Near

Day 2: Overcoming Worry

Day 3: To Strengthen

Day 4: Armor of God

Day 5: Truth and Righteousness

Day 6   Peace and Faith

Day 7: Salvation and Spirit

DAY ONE

Draw Near

Many people blame God for the consequences of their sin; they accuse Him of tempting them and allowing them to give in. To set the record straight: God may allow our faith to be tested and refined, but He never leads us to sin. That's the devil's job, and he does it well. Satan tempts us with the intent of luring us away from God's goodness and purity. He doesn't need to be very creative in his efforts; he entices us by using our own desires to lead us astray. Even though we have been forgiven for our sins and are filled with the Holy Spirit, we still have a battle with our flesh to contend against. The apostle Paul addresses this struggle in **Romans 7:14-25**. This amazing hero of the faith admits that his words and actions don't always align with his new identity in Christ. He is aware of the battle and faces it head on. He finds strength and encouragement by delighting himself in God's Law. We find strength by reading our Bibles too. The more we store God's Word in our hearts, the more aware of sin we become and the more effective we are at resisting temptation.

James 1:13-15 holds us accountable for our own choices: *"When tempted, no one should say, 'God is tempting me.' For God cannot be tempted by evil, nor does he tempt anyone; ¹⁴ but each person is tempted when they are dragged away by their own evil desire and enticed. ¹⁵ Then, after desire has conceived, it gives birth to sin; and sin, when it is full-grown, gives birth to death."*

1 Corinthians 10:13 NLT, *"The temptations in your life are no different from what others experience. And God is faithful. He will not allow the temptation to be more than you can stand. When you are tempted, he will show you a way out so that you can endure."*

Any time sin begins to stir in our hearts and occupy our minds, we have a conscious decision to make—be led astray or choose to pursue the godly way. Often when we come to a fork in the road, one path will lead us to blessing and the other quite possibly to destruction **(Deuteronomy 11:26-28)**. The path of blessing requires drawing near to God in submission to His plan—He gladly shows us the way. It demands that we resist the devil and his enticements. In all this the Holy Spirit is our helper! We need only listen and obey.

"Thanks be to God, who delivers me through Jesus Christ our Lord!" Romans 7:25

James 4:7-8 tells us to, *"Submit yourselves, then, to God. Resist the devil, and he will flee from you. ⁸ Come near to God and he will come near to you. Wash your hands, you sinners, and purify your hearts, you double-minded."*

1. Satan plays on your weakness when attempting to lead you astray. Are you aware of certain times or situations when you're more vulnerable—tired, hungry, angry, bitter, resentful, jealous, insecure about yourself? When you're around certain people? Honestly explain.

2. How can you draw near to God in these situations? How can you prepare to resist the devil? It's good to come up with a plan ahead of time.

Before going to the Cross, Jesus prayed to His Heavenly Father. He also encouraged His disciples saying: *"Watch and pray so that you will not fall into temptation. The spirit is willing, but the flesh is weak."* **(Matthew 26:41)**. If Jesus told His disciples to pray to resist temptation, then we should pray this way too. Begin by acknowledging your struggles to the Lord. Ask Him to strengthen your spirit.

Lord, I submit myself to You. Please show me the way out of temptation.

Amen.

DAY TWO

Overcoming Worry

Raise your hand if you ever worry. Yep, me too—although we shouldn't allow it to consume us. Worry runs contrary to our faith and is in opposition of what God desires for us. Our worry, anxiety, and depression must be confessed and surrendered to the Lord. Otherwise, they will lead us to troubled places where we should not wander. The Lord sacrificed His life to set us free; but we must consciously choose to walk in that freedom. Sometimes it's a daily choice, while other times it's a prolonged season of endurance. We must give it to God again and again, no matter how many times it takes. He won't deliver us from something we refuse to acknowledge or let go of. The Lord does not tempt us to worry, doubt, or fear, rather He invites us to trust in Him.

Daniel was thrown into a lion's den where he calmly spent the night aware of God's Presence **(Daniel 6)**. Three young Israelite men refused to worship the king and confidently entered a fiery furnace **(Daniel 3)**. They all refused to bow down to their worries or be taken captive by fear. They gave their allegiance to the Lord and trusted Him completely. They resisted the devil and his schemes to overtake them. They knew that God had the power to rescue them and entrusted themselves to His protection. They could have worried and panicked; they could have compromised their faith, but they didn't. Their testimony of resistance, resilience, and faith is still inspiring us today.

Jesus addressed the issue of worry and explained how useless and harmful it can be. The devil would love for us to take the bait and feel hopeless, helpless, and to endlessly spin our wheels, but Jesus teaches us a better way—He says, *do not worry*. He reminds us that *God cares for the flowers and the birds*. We are given this assurance: *how much more will He care for you* **(Matthew 6:25-34)**. Worry cannot fix anything or add any more hours to our day; it only steals precious moments from our life one burden at a time. The schemes of the enemy are often very sly—he wants to keep us preoccupied with anxiety so that we lose focus of the Lord and His promises. The devil knows that worry paralyzes us with irrational fears and renders us ineffective for the Lord's purpose. He wants to steal the joy that is rightfully ours as a child of God. We don't have to allow him; we can hold tight to our blessings **(Revelation 3:11-12)**. God gave them to us for keeps!

"When anxiety was great within me, your consolation brought me joy." Psalm 94:19

Let's resist the temptation to worry by taking our thoughts captive and making them obedient to Christ and focusing on truth **(2 Corinthians 10:5; Philippians 4:6-8)**. Let's hand our concerns over to the Lord before they begin to snowball into something bigger than they really are—He can handle it. God is on the throne, let's live like we believe it! Ask Him to give you His perspective.

"Cast all your anxiety on him because he cares for you." 1 Peter 5:7

1. Please read **Matthew 6:25-34** to hear Jesus' exhortation on worry. What does Jesus say we should seek first and why **(6:33)**? How can this ease our anxieties?

2. Read **Philippians 4:6-8** and write out God's prescription for overcoming anxiety.

What specific concern is weighing heavy on your heart and mind? God can help before it grows any bigger. He will lead you away from temptation and deliver you from the prison of worry. Ask Him to fill you with peace and to protect you now. Persist in this prayer until it is answered. Worshipping the Lord also lifts our eyes above our circumstances.

Heavenly Father, You know what I need,

Amen.

DAY THREE

To Strengthen

While Satan roams the earth seeking someone to devour, God's eyes range throughout the world with the intent of strengthening His children. What a comfort and consolation to know that God has not left us to deal with our struggles alone. Far too often we think we must self-will ourselves to be strong and courageous, to face those dreadful demons, overcome our past, and resist temptation, but this is not the case. **Philippians 4:13** reminds us, *"I can do all this through him who gives me strength."* The Lord of Heaven and earth offers to shore up our souls, strengthen our spirits, redirect our minds, lead us in truth, and guide our lives. When we invite the Lord to strengthen us, we also find peace that surpasses our understanding **(Psalm 29:11; Philippians 4:7)**. To enjoy these blessings and experience these benefits, we must first surrender and fully commit our hearts to Him and seek His ways.

> *"For the eyes of the* LORD *range throughout the earth to strengthen those whose hearts are fully committed to him."* 2 Chronicles 16:9

God's divine power is at work for, in, and through His dear people if we permit Him access. We have the option to keep control for ourselves, but that is never a good idea. Instead, we would be wise to whole-heartedly trust in our Savior. Our knowledge of God and His authority, glory, love, and mercy, combined with our understanding of our identity in Christ, equips us for every challenge and hurdle we face. The Lord has not left us as orphans, but continually reaches out with the purpose of guiding and nurturing His children—sometimes that includes dispensing His loving discipline. God is in our corner, desiring that we overcome temptation and choose His path forward—in every decision. Our choices include what words to speak and what actions to take—God wants to be at the center of it all. Everything begins with the focus of our hearts and minds. Strength is found in the Lord's presence. God is for us **(Romans 8:31)**. Amen!

> *"His divine power has given us everything we need for a godly life through our knowledge of him who called us by his own glory and goodness."* 2 Peter 1:3

God has given us His Holy Spirit to dwell in our hearts, and His Holy Word to reveal His ways. We overcome temptation and walk in deliverance from evil, by praying in the Spirit, searching our Bibles for truth, and leaning into His mighty power.

1. **Psalm 119** is the longest chapter in the Bible, having 176 verses. It shares the key to freedom and lasting happiness—something we all desire. Read the following portions of **Psalm 119:1-48, 105-106**. Throughout his meditations, the Psalmist uses expressions such as: *law, statutes, precepts, commands, decrees*, to represent God's Word. This is the focus of his heart. How does God's Word bless, strengthen, and guide you? Is it your focus?

2. Take a moment to read **Isaiah 40:28-31.** Describe God's strength, and then write out **verse 40:31**.

Confess your hope in the Lord and ask Him to help you soar above your troubles, your worries, your fears, your past transgressions, and your present temptations. Ask Him to renew your strength, endurance, and power to overcome.

Lord, You are the everlasting God and Creator. Help me soar on wings like eagles.

Amen.

DAY FOUR

Armor of God

God has not left us uninformed, unequipped, or ill-prepared. He has exposed the devil as our true enemy and revealed the real source of our battle. He has also shown us how we must fight—not in our own strength, but in His mighty power.

Ephesians 6:10-18, *"Finally, be strong in the Lord and in his mighty power. [11] Put on the full armor of God, so that you can take your stand against the devil's schemes. [12] For our struggle is not against flesh and blood, but against the rulers, against the authorities, against the powers of this dark world and against the spiritual forces of evil in the heavenly realms. [13] Therefore put on the full armor of God, so that when the day of evil comes, you may be able to stand your ground, and after you have done everything, to stand. [14] Stand firm then, with the belt of truth buckled around your waist, with the breastplate of righteousness in place, [15] and with your feet fitted with the readiness that comes from the gospel of peace. [16] In addition to all this, take up the shield of faith, with which you can extinguish all the flaming arrows of the evil one. [17] Take the helmet of salvation and the sword of the Spirit, which is the word of God. [18] And pray in the Spirit on all occasions with all kinds of prayers and requests. With this in mind, be alert and always keep on praying for all the Lord's people."*

We have been given God's armor to wear. It is not something we have to piece together on our own. His armor provides everything we could possibly need in fighting our battles—which at their root are spiritual. It may feel as if our battle is with our current situation, or the person who's standing in our way or inflicting pain in our lives; but truly the attacks we face are coming straight from the devil. **The Book of Revelation (verse 6:2)** reveals the climax of God's story. Someday Jesus will return, riding in as a conqueror upon a white horse, finally putting an end to death, sin, and Satan once and for all time. When we place our faith in Jesus, we join the victorious side. We are rescued from the dominion of darkness and brought into the Kingdom of Light **(Colossians 1:11-14)**. We become citizens and even heirs in God's family **(Ephesians 2:19; Romans 8:17)**. The devil no longer has authority over us, and we become more than conquerors in Christ **(Romans 8:37-39)**. Although we stand triumphantly with Jesus, Satan will try to dissuade, discourage, and defeat us on a daily basis. The armor of God has many pieces that fit perfectly together—providing protection for our spirit, mind, and heart. God's Word describes and then gives us instructions on how to utilize each piece.

1. I would like you to reread the **Ephesians 6:10-18** passage, and then list every piece of armor here:

2. Now list every action word or phrase you find. These verbs apply to you.

The Lord offers us His armor, but it is up to us to put it on and utilize it. This is not a one-time action—we must consciously wear it every day. The enemy won't stop his assaults, so we should always be prepared. Wearing God's armor is essential to our standing firm. Ask the Lord to strengthen you in His Mighty Power.

Dear Lord,

Amen.

DAY FIVE

Truth and Righteousness

For the remainder of the week, we will look more closely at each item of God's armor. We will discover how the pieces fit together and how they can positively impact our lives. God's armor is unlike any earthly arsenal—it gives us supernatural power to stand firm in our faith and walk triumphantly on this earth.

"Therefore put on the full armor of God, so that when the day of evil comes, you may be able to stand your ground, and after you have done everything, to stand."

Ephesians 6:13

Today we will address the first two components of the Lord's armor—there is a purposeful order to putting them on. The first and foundational article is the belt of truth, and the second essential element is the breastplate of righteousness.

"Stand firm then, with the belt of truth buckled around your waist, with the breastplate of righteousness in place..." Ephesians 6:14

The NKJV states it this way: *"Stand therefore, having girded your waist with truth, having put on the breastplate of righteousness..."* Girding our waist means being ready for action, and the battlefield provides us with plenty of that. There is a good reason for putting *truth* first—it affects every successive piece. If our truth is askew, then our armor will be faulty. Our truth must be founded on the Word of God. We must believe that Jesus Christ is Lord and that He is the only way to the Father. We must choose to follow God's truth above personal opinion or the world's philosophies. Satan would love to persuade people into believing anything other than the Bible—and he does a good job at it if we're not careful. The more familiar we are with Scripture, the less likely we are to fall victim to his schemes. Stand firm and be ready for action with biblical truth as your protection!

The breastplate of righteousness is directly linked to our idea of truth. We know that Jesus is our Lord, and we trust Him as Savior—He freed us from sin and released us from condemnation. That is truth! Being that we have been forgiven, our grateful response is to choose to live His way—and that is in righteousness. Every time we sin, Satan is given an opportunity to gain a foothold over us. It's as if we've given him a personal invitation to wreak havoc in our lives. This is obviously something we'd like to avoid. The breastplate of righteousness covers all our vital organs, most importantly it protects our heart. Sin is destructive and God wants to protect us from its repercussions. Putting on the breastplate of righteousness means steering clear of sin and choosing holiness in the face of temptation. I can just hear the devil's angry outcry when we allow righteousness to guide our decisions. Protect your heart because it is the doorway to everything else in your life. Walk in righteousness and seal your armor up tight. Don't give the enemy access, rather surrender your life to Christ.

1. Please read **John 8:31-32**. What does truth accomplish for us?

2. Now read **Ephesians 4:17-24** and then write out verses **4:23-24**. What were we *created to be like*?

Pray and thank God for giving you His armor and equipping you for battle. Ask Him to help you remember to wear it every day.

Dear Heavenly Father,

Amen.

DAY SIX

Peace and Faith

The armor of God comes together one item at a time, to cover us from head to toe with God's holy protection. So far, the belt of truth is securely fastened and readying us for action; and the breastplate of righteousness is protecting us from sin and sealing our hearts for God's Kingdom. The next two articles we must adorn ourselves with are the *shoes of peace* and the *shield of faith*. Peace and faith have amazing power to help us overcome temptation and deliver us from evil.

> *"And with your feet fitted with the readiness that comes from the gospel of peace. ¹⁶ In addition to all this, take up the shield of faith, with which you can extinguish all the flaming arrows of the evil one." Ephesians 6:15-16*

Feet are very important parts of the body—they support our weight and take us where we need to go. They carry us up hills and through deep valleys. They can also lead us into temptation or move us closer to the Lord. What we wear on our feet matters. Shoes full of pebbles cause us to hobble; ill-fitting sandals will cause us to stumble. The older I get the more important my footwear choices become, and they seem to affect my whole well-being. They can cause me to wince in pain or float on clouds of comfort. I'm continually searching for the perfect pair of shoes—and God has designed the ones that suit every occasion.

The NKJV phrases **Ephesians 6:15** this way: *"having shod your feet with the preparation of the gospel of peace..."* The Greek meaning of the words *"having shod"* is *to bind under one's feet*. What a beautiful picture of strapping our feet securely to the Gospel of Peace—walking in a state of peace wherever we go. Through Jesus' sacrifice on the Cross, our relationship with God has been restored—that is the Gospel of Peace at the core! We now enjoy peace with our Heavenly Father **(Colossians 1:20)**. On top of that, we also get to experience the peace of God in our everyday lives. While obstacles arise and troubles pop up, we can walk assuredly knowing that God is in control **(Philippians 4:7)**. Panic won't be allowed to get the better of us and Satan can't knock us off balance when our feet are shod with God's peace. The peace of God which is found in the Gospel should guide our steps and inform our choices and reactions. Our peace is also a testimony to others—notice is taken when we aren't easily rattled or shaken—our peace points to God. Remember to lace up your shoes of peace today!

Our next essential piece of armor is the *shield of faith*. I'm sure you've felt the fiery darts of the enemy whizzing past you and have even incurred injury from his direct aim. Satan knows exactly which arrows to shoot and at the right time—he's very opportunistic. He continually hurls doubt, insecurity, fear, shame, bitterness, and temptation in our direction. Faith is our shield no matter what comes at us. Choosing to believe God and trusting that He is good, is a surefire way of extinguishing the flames headed our way. They fizzle to the ground before reaching our heart. The shield of faith enables us to believe God's promises over what we see or feel.

1. According to **John 16:33**, how do we find peace? How does this help you take heart?

2. Looking at **Colossians 1:4-5**, where does faith spring from? Is *your* hope in Christ translating to faith in Him daily too?

Ask the Lord to help you walk in His peace and utilize His shield of faith.

Dear Lord,

Amen.

DAY SEVEN

Salvation and Spirit

"Take the helmet of salvation and the sword of the Spirit, which is the word of God. ¹⁸ And pray in the Spirit on all occasions with all kinds of prayers and requests. With this in mind, be alert and always keep on praying for all the Lord's people."

Ephesians 6:17-18

Two keys to being an overcomer are knowing our identity in Christ and keeping God's Word stored in our hearts. Putting on the helmet of salvation daily means remembering all the benefits we have received through our relationship with Jesus—we are chosen, redeemed, included, and we have been sealed with the Holy Spirit. We have the promise that God is with us every day, and the hope of Heaven on the horizon. We are children of God—sons, and daughters of the King of kings. This realization should cause us to guard our hearts and set our minds on heavenly things. It should spur us on toward righteousness and strongly caution us against sin. We should be filled with confidence in our standing before God and courage as we encounter trials of many kinds. Protecting our minds with the helmet of salvation denies the enemy a foothold and ensures that he cannot lead us astray with his lies. We are who God says we are—beloved heirs in His mighty Kingdom!

"And you also were included in Christ when you heard the message of truth, the gospel of your salvation. When you believed, you were marked in him with a seal, the promised Holy Spirit," Ephesians 1:13

The sword of the Spirit is an essential component to our armor—it is the Word of God, the unchanging truth by which we measure all things. God's Word has the power to redirect, encourage, empower us, and put the devil in his place. It must be stored in our hearts so that it can be readily accessed. Jesus used the sword of the Spirit to refute the devil and rebuke his temptations. He confidently overcame

Satan's offers with Scripture, beginning each of His statements with the words, *"it is written."* He didn't struggle with His response; He stood unwaveringly on His Father's promises **(Matthew 4:1-11)**. We can and should respond likewise. The Word of God should fill our minds and saturate our hearts. It should spring from our lips in response to tempting situations.

"As for God, his way is perfect: The LORD's word is flawless; he shields all who take refuge in him." Psalm 18:30

1. Please read **Philippians 2:15-16** and record the importance of holding *firmly to the word of life*, which is the Bible.

2. How will *the helmet of salvation* and *the sword of the Spirit* better equip you to live more victoriously?

Temptation is a fork in the road where we decide which way to go. The Lord always provides a way out, but it is up to us to select His option. **We are born again of the Spirit, and He is our teacher and guide. We are exhorted to pray on all occasions and be alert at all times. So, let's do that now.**

Dear Lord, help me to remember who I am and to claim Your Word in my life.

Amen.

"I call on you, my God, for you will answer me;

turn your ear to me and hear my prayer.

⁷ Show me the wonders of your great love,

you who save by your right hand

those who take refuge in you from their foes.

⁸ Keep me as the apple of your eye;

hide me in the shadow of your wings

⁹ from the wicked who are out to destroy me,

from my mortal enemies who surround me." Psalm 17:6-9

WEEK EIGHT

Prayer Prompts

"For this reason, I kneel before the Father..." Ephesians 3:14

Day 1: Jesus' Springboard

Day 2: A.C.T.S. Acronym

Day 3: Ask, Seek, Knock

Day 4: Watch and Pray

Day 5: Joyful, Patient, Faithful

Day 6: Prayer, Petition, Thanksgiving

Day 7: Rejoice, Pray, Give Thanks

This week offers an opportunity for you to pray a bit more independently. I have provided simple *prayer prompts* to inspire your thoughts and words. I pray that the Spirit moves you and that the promises of the Bible come to mind and spring to life for you too. I hope that inspiration flows onto the page as you present your praise, worship, and requests to the Lord. Don't hesitate or overthink it, just listen to the Lord and speak honestly from your heart.

Before you begin, I'd like to focus our hearts and minds on God's character and His names on which we can rely. They may inspire your worship and instill confidence as you bring your requests to Him.

God is: holy, righteous, just, loving, kind, merciful, gracious, powerful, and strong. The Lord is: infinite, eternal, immutable, omnipresent, omniscient, omnipotent, all-sufficient, and sovereign.

The following are some of God's names that we can cry out to as various situations and needs arise: He is Creator, Sustainer, Great Physician, King of kings, Lord of lords, The Great I AM, The Alpha and Omega, God Almighty, Everlasting Father. He is the God who sees. Jesus is the Good Shepherd, the Lamb of God, Son of the Most High, The Word, Bread of Life, and Living Water. He is our Redeemer, Savior, Provider, Rewarder, Wonderful Counselor, and Prince of Peace. *Jesus* means: *the Lord saves. Emmanuel* is: *God with us* **(Matthew 1:23)**.

Which characteristic of God do you need to praise? Which attribute do you need to call on to meet your current needs?

Now that we have laid a firm and essential foundation of who our prayers are directed to, I'd like to share some verses that stress the importance of prayer in our lives:

Romans 12:12, "Be joyful in hope, patient in affliction, faithful in prayer."

Ephesians 6:18-19, "And pray in the Spirit on all occasions with all kinds of prayers and requests. With this in mind, be alert and always keep on praying for all the Lord's people. [19] Pray also for me, that whenever I speak, words may be given me so that I will fearlessly make known the mystery of the gospel,"

Philippians 1:9, "And this is my prayer: that your love may abound more and more in knowledge and depth of insight,"

Philippians 4:6, "Do not be anxious about anything, but in every situation, by prayer and petition, with thanksgiving, present your requests to God."

Colossians 1:9, "For this reason, since the day we heard about you, we have not stopped praying for you. We continually ask God to fill you with the knowledge of his will through all the wisdom and understanding that the Spirit gives,"

Colossians 4:2-4, "Devote yourselves to prayer, being watchful and thankful. [3] And pray for us, too, that God may open a door for our message, so that we may proclaim the mystery of Christ, for which I am in chains. [4] Pray that I may proclaim it clearly, as I should."

Colossians 4:12, "Epaphras...is always wrestling in prayer for you, that you may stand firm in all the will of God, mature and fully assured."

1 Thessalonians 5:17, "pray continually,"

2 Thessalonians 1:3, "We ought always to thank God for you, brothers and sisters, and rightly so, because your faith is growing more and more, and the love all of you have for one another is increasing."

2 Thessalonians 3:1-2, "Pray for us that the message of the Lord may spread rapidly and be honored, just as it was with you. [2] And pray that we may be delivered from wicked and evil people, for not everyone has faith."

1 Timothy 2:1, "I urge, then, first of all, that petitions, prayers, intercession and thanksgiving be made for all people—"

James 5:13-18, "Is anyone among you in trouble? Let them pray. Is anyone happy? Let them sing songs of praise. [14] Is anyone among you sick? Let them call the elders of the church to pray over them and anoint them with oil in the name of the Lord. [15] And the prayer offered in faith will make the sick person well; the Lord will raise them up. If they have sinned, they will be forgiven. [16] Therefore confess your sins to each other and pray for each other so that you may be healed. The prayer of a righteous person is powerful and effective. [17] Elijah was a human being, even as we are. He prayed earnestly that it would not rain, and it did not rain on the land for three and a half years. [18] Again he prayed, and the heavens gave rain, and the earth produced its crops."

1 Peter 4:7, "The end of all things is near. Therefore be alert and of sober mind so that you may pray."

Jude 20-21, "But you, dear friends, by building yourselves up in your most holy faith and praying in the Holy Spirit, [21] keep yourselves in God's love as you wait for the mercy of our Lord Jesus Christ to bring you to eternal life."

DAY ONE

Jesus' Springboard

Matthew 6:9-13

Our Father in heaven, hallowed be your name...

Your kingdom come, your will be done, on earth as it is in heaven...

Give us today our daily bread...

And forgive us our debts, as we also have forgiven our debtors...

And lead us not into temptation, but deliver us from the evil one...

DAY TWO

A.C.T.S.

A Simple Acronym

Adoration: I offer You all my praise and worship...

Confession: Lord, I confess my sins, my flaws, and my need for a Savior...

Thanksgiving: I am so thankful for Your mercies that are new every morning...

Supplication: I lay my requests, my cares, my needs, and my burdens before You...

DAY THREE

Ask, Seek, Knock

Matthew 7:7-8

Ask: Lord, I am asking for...

Seek: Lord, I will keep seeking...

Knock: Lord, I am persistently knocking...

DAY FOUR

Watch and Pray

Matthew 26:41

Watch: Lord, help me to be alert and watchful; please guard and protect me...

Pray: Lord, search my heart and hear my prayers...

DAY FIVE

Joyful, Patient, Faithful

Romans 12:12

Joyful: Heavenly Father, these are the reasons for my joy...

Please help me to experience Your joy more fully...

Patient: Lord, thank You for Your patience with me....

Help me to be patient in the process and in the waiting...

Faithful: You God, are faithful to me....

Help me to walk faithfully with You...

DAY SIX

Prayer, Petition, Thanksgiving

Philippians 4:6

Prayer: Lord, hear my prayers...

Petitions: These are the petitions of my heart...

Thanksgiving: I am so grateful for...

DAY SEVEN

Rejoice, Pray, Give Thanks

1 Thessalonians 5:16-18

Rejoice: Lord, I rejoice in Your Presence...

Pray: I come before Your Throne and pray...

Give Thanks: I give thanks for all my blessings—my hope, peace, love, and joy...

WEEK NINE

Prayer Devotions

"By day the LORD *directs his love, at night his song is with me—a prayer to the God of my life." Psalm 42:8*

Day 1:   Our Light

Day 2:   Our Shield

Day 3:   Our Refuge

Day 4:   Our Comfort

Day 5:   His Fruit

Day 6:   His Love

Day 7:   His Dwelling Place

DAY ONE

Our Light

"In the beginning God created the heavens and the earth." Genesis 1:1

Dear Heavenly Father,

You are Creator of heaven and earth, and You alone rule in authority over Your creation. You brought order to the chaos of the cosmos, and You continue to bring peace to our lives. You have purpose for everything, and You give meaning to everyone who has been crafted by Your mighty hands. You created us for the very specific reason of having a relationship with You. All of creation testifies to Your goodness and the galaxies declare Your glory. You separated the light from the darkness with just Your spoken Word. You placed the stars in the heavens and made the moon and sun to shine in the sky. You sent Jesus to be our true Light, shining the way and leading us into Your welcoming arms. Your light and love radiate in our hearts and warm our very souls. Thank You, Lord, for taking us out of the darkness and bringing us into Your Heavenly Kingdom.

Amen.

"While I am in the world, I am the light of the world." John 9:5

"Through him all things were made; without him nothing was made that has been made. ⁴ In him was life, and that life was the light of all mankind. ⁵ The light shines in the darkness, and the darkness has not overcome it." John 1:3-5

For further inspiration open your Bible to read **Psalm 104:1-35** and then write out your own prayer to your loving and all-powerful Creator.

Prayer and Notes:

DAY TWO

Our Shield

"My shield is God Most High, who saves the upright in heart." Psalm 7:10

God Most High,

You are the God who blesses, delivers, and provides. You alone are worthy of our worship. Every good and perfect gift comes from Your sovereign hand. You give us victory over our enemies and show us favor in the land. When evil seems to triumph, we need only to remember that You still rule from Your throne above. You are always in complete control; nothing occurs outside of Your knowledge or permission. Lord, help me to keep my eyes on You; to walk through every valley knowing that You are with me; to come out to the other side and stand on the mountaintop with You. Your plans for me are always good and thank goodness they always prevail. You pave the way before me; You hold my hand and walk beside me; You guard me from behind. You deliver me from evil and send angels to defend me. You are my safe, strong tower. You divinely hedge me in on all sides. Everything I have and all that I am, belongs to You. I am grateful that You are God Most High, sovereign over this world—and me. Meditating on You and Your promises to sustain me brings indescribable peace that passes all understanding.

Amen.

"Whoever dwells in the shelter of the Most High will rest in the shadow of the Almighty." Psalm 91:1

2 Samuel 22:1-20 recounts the numerous ways that God Most High reached down from Heaven to rescue David. This is the same God who rescues you and me. I encourage you to read this passage and ask God to bring you into *spacious places*.

Prayer and Notes:

DAY THREE

Our Refuge

"LORD Almighty, blessed is the one who trusts in you." Psalm 84:12

Lord Almighty,

There is no one like You. You alone are holy, righteous, perfect, and good in all Your ways. You are my strength, my deliverer, my guard, and my rock. You are the God of Israel—faithful to your promises and to Your people. You are God to those who place their faith in Jesus. You discipline those You love to bring about Your good purpose. You compassionately refresh the weary and satisfy those faint of heart and body. You are the God of Heaven, reigning from Your throne above. You are in authority over the days and seasons, over kings and leaders, and over every breath I take. You know and see all things past, present, and future. You are the source of all wisdom and power, and You give knowledge of Your ways and strength to those who earnestly seek You. You are our refuge and comfort in times of trouble. I fully trust in You. Thank you, Lord, for making Yourself known and allowing us to ascend Your holy mountain where blessings are found in Your presence. Lord, I want more of You!

Amen.

"Taste and see that the LORD is good; blessed is the one who takes refuge in Him."

Psalm 34:8

"Those who seek the Lord lack no good thing." The Lord has everything we need. His blessings are abundant, lavish, and exquisite. They are priceless and life-giving. He answers, He delivers, He rescues, He is close, and He saves. Read **Psalm 34:1-22** to learn more about the Lord's generosity towards those who love Him and take refuge in Him. Tell the Lord what these blessings mean to you.

Prayer and Notes:

DAY FOUR

Our Comfort

"She gave this name to the LORD who spoke to her: 'You are the God who sees me,' for she said, 'I have now seen the One who sees me.'" Genesis 16:13

Dear Lord,

You are the God who sees me. You saw me in my mother's womb when no one even yet knew I existed. You have seen every moment of my life, and You never cease to be with me. All the days of my life past, present, and future are laid out before You and recorded in Your book. There is nothing about me that escapes Your notice or care. You have numbered the hairs on my head and kept a record of all my tears. You are the God who sees, hears, cares, and acts on my behalf. Please open my eyes and make me aware of Your continual nearness. Remind me that I am never alone, never forgotten, never overlooked, or disregarded. Help me to feel Your strong arms around me, to hear Your comforting words in my ears. Open my eyes to Your constant presence. You are my help and my hope, and You calm my fears. Thank You, Lord.

Amen.

"And even the very hairs of your head are all numbered." Matthew 10:30

Psalm 119:145-152 reminds us that the Lord is near, and His commands are true. Every word that comes from our Father's mouth is meant to preserve our life and fortify our soul. God is good all the time and He showers His goodness on us. When we call out to Him, He saves us. I encourage you to read **Psalm 119:145-152** for yourself and then pray accordingly.

Prayer and Notes:

DAY FIVE

His Fruit

"And this is my prayer: that your love may abound more and more in knowledge and depth of insight, ⁱ⁰ so that you may be able to discern what is best and may be pure and blameless for the day of Christ, ¹¹filled with the fruit of righteousness that comes through Jesus Christ—to the glory and praise of God." Philippians 1:9-11

The Bible is filled with beautiful prayers written by godly people. Their words may have been spoken and recorded centuries ago, but they still perfectly apply to us today. Their prayers and petitions often inspire the content of my own—I may alter the phrasing but the meaning behind them remains the same. You can use the apostle Paul's prayer from Philippians to inspire your own supplication too.

O Lord,

This is my prayer too. I pray to know and more fully understand Your love for me and for every human being You have created. I pray that as a result, my love for others will grow and overflow in Your Name. Please expand the love You have poured into my heart until I can no longer contain it. May I be Your vessel of mercy and grace in this world. Help me to choose what is good, pure, and right according to Your Word. Give me discernment to recognize what is best and what is harmful. Help me to clearly see the difference between right and wrong, good and evil, light and dark. I pray this not only for myself, but also for my loved ones. Keep us safe from evil and fill us with the fruit of righteousness—this is only possible because Your Spirit continually works to refine us. Thank You God for not leaving us alone but for walking this journey with us. Teach us Your ways, show us Your path, use our lives to glorify and bring You praise. Thank You, Lord God Almighty, every good and perfect gift is from Your hand!

Amen.

Prayer and Notes:

DAY SIX

His Love

"I pray that out of his glorious riches he may strengthen you with power through his Spirit in your inner being, [17] so that Christ may dwell in your hearts through faith. And I pray that you, being rooted and established in love, [18] may have power, together with all the Lord's holy people, to grasp how wide and long and high and deep is the love of Christ, [19] and to know this love that surpasses knowledge—that you may be filled to the measure of all the fullness of God. [20] Now to him who is able to do immeasurably more than all we ask or imagine, according to his power that is at work within us, [21] to him be glory in the church and in Christ Jesus throughout all generations, for ever and ever! Amen." Ephesians 3:16-21

This is one of my favorite prayers in the Bible. Knowing God's love changes everything for a person. I pray this prayer for myself, and I also insert the names of family members and friends who need to know God's love for them. The love of God is the firm foundation on which we can plant our feet; it is the anchor our restless souls need. We crave love, and God is the One who can satisfy that longing. God is love and all love emanates from Him. I have written a prayer based on Paul's words and I encourage you to do the same. Pray for yourself and for individuals in your life to know Jesus and the love God has for them.

"This is how God showed his love among us: He sent his one and only Son into the world that we might live through him. [10] This is love: not that we loved God, but that he loved us and sent his Son as an atoning sacrifice for our sins." 1 John 4:9-10

God Almighty,

Heaven holds a storehouse of riches that are far beyond my comprehension. You have everything I could possibly need for daily living, as I await Your coming Kingdom. All glory and honor belong to You. All strength and power are found in You. I place my life in Your capable hands and entrust myself to Your loving care. I believe that You are good, merciful, gracious, and kind; You are sovereign, holy, righteous, and just. I choose to walk by faith and not by sight. I know that You love me, but sometimes I put Your love in a box—yet really Your love is bigger and greater than I can truly fathom. Help me to grasp just how enormous Your love for me is—give me this supernatural revelation. Remind me to always look to the Cross, for it reveals how high and deep and wide Your love is for me and all of humanity. Your love reached down from the heights of Heaven to the earth far below. Your love is demonstrated through arms stretched wide at Jesus' crucifixion. You sacrificed Your Son for me. Help me to understand this love better. I know that love is the essence of who You are, and it changes everything for all those who encounter it! Fill me to the fullness of everything You have to offer. I come to You in prayer knowing that You have all the answers. Your power is at work in me, doing amazing things for Your glory. I pray that Your love will become tangibly real for me; that it floods my heart and fills every bit of my life. I pray these things not only for myself, but for my family and friends as well. I know that Your love has the power to transform lives, and I want this for all my loved ones. Give them a revelation of the enormity of Your love too! Thank You, Lord God, for who You are!

Amen.

Begin your prayer here and go onto the next page if needed. Add to your prayer as more loved ones who need to encounter God's love come to mind. Continue praying for God to reveal Himself and He will, in His perfect way and His sovereign timing.

Prayer and Notes:

DAY SEVEN

His Dwelling Place

"How lovely is your dwelling place, LORD Almighty! ² My soul yearns, even faints, for the courts of the LORD; my heart and my flesh cry out for the living God. ³ Even the sparrow has found a home, and the swallow a nest for herself, where she may have her young—a place near your altar, LORD Almighty, my King and my God. ⁴ Blessed are those who dwell in your house; they are ever praising you. ⁵ Blessed are those whose strength is in you, whose hearts are set on pilgrimage. ⁶ As they pass through the Valley of Baka, they make it a place of springs; the autumn rains also cover it with pools. ⁷ They go from strength to strength, till each appears before God in Zion. ⁸ Hear my prayer, LORD God Almighty; listen to me, God of Jacob. ⁹ Look on our shield, O God; look with favor on your anointed one. ¹⁰ Better is one day in your courts than a thousand elsewhere; I would rather be a doorkeeper in the house of my God than dwell in the tents of the wicked. ¹¹ For the LORD God is a sun and shield; the LORD bestows favor and honor; no good thing does he withhold from those whose walk is blameless. ¹² LORD Almighty, blessed is the one who trusts in you."
Psalm 84: 1-12

God's Word is truly inspiring! I have written a prayer in response to the psalmist's sentiments, and I invite you to do the same. Pour out your heart and tell God exactly what He means to you. Praise Him, thank Him, and ask Him to meet your longings with His perfect satisfaction.

Dear Lord,

The psalmist who penned these words writes from personal experience—day after day he ministered in Your holy Temple, and he knows the privilege of being in Your presence. He has entered Your rest, he has felt Your love, experienced Your protection, and enjoyed Your blessings. His words perfectly represent the cries of my heart and eloquently express the thoughts that are sometimes hard for me to describe. To reside in Your glorious presence is my deepest desire and my greatest joy. Being close to You Lord, is the realization of true peace, hope, love, and joy. You are the fulfillment of my every longing and the end of all my searching—with You I find contentment. You are the source of every blessing that's worth pursuing. My soul yearns to be near to You—truly, there is nothing better. Thank you, Lord, for inviting me into your lovely dwelling place; It is where I feel most at home.

Amen.

Reread **Psalm 84:1-12** and then author a prayer to the Lord for yourself.

Prayer and Notes:

Closing Encouragement

Our time together has come to an end, but your journey with the Lord continues forever. My hope is that you keep opening your Bible with the intent of hearing from God, and that you persevere in coming to the Lord in prayer. God is speaking, we need only listen; God is listening, we need only share our joys, cares, and concerns. We can pray for and about anything that is laid on our hearts or weighing on our minds. We should praise God for His holiness and thank Him for His goodness to us. We can tell Him our troubles, ask Him for healing, guidance, and Divine intervention. God holds the power and with love He extends it. He invites us into sweet and ongoing fellowship with Him. He is before all things, in all things, and He has the answers we need. His Presence goes with us wherever we wander. He is our refuge in times of trouble. He is our source of security and confidence in this world. He has promised to be with us now and has promised to return for us so we can be with Him for all eternity. Our hope is in the Lord—He has proven His love and faithfulness to us through the sacrifice of His Son Jesus Christ.

The Bible is full of promises and encouragements for us to claim and cling to. Keep reading. Keep praying. Continue journaling your prayers of worship and petition. Your relationship with the Lord is the key to a fulfilling life. Thank you for spending this time with me. Even if we never meet in person, know that I am praying for you.

Love & blessings, Tracy

> "The LORD bless you and keep you;
>
> [25] the LORD make his face shine on you
>
> and be gracious to you;
>
> [26] the LORD turn his face toward you
>
> and give you peace.'" Numbers 6:24-26

"I call to you, LORD, come quickly to me;

hear me when I call to you.

²May my prayer be set before you like incense;

may the lifting up of my hands be like the evening sacrifice."

Psalm 141:1-2

Leader Guide

Suggestions for Small Group Discussions

My summary videos are designed to be watched after you have completed your homework each week. The videos can be found on:
www.youtube.com/@beblessedandinspiredwithtracy/videos

Introduction—Here are a few ideas to help get you started:

1. Grab a coffee, get comfy, open in prayer, and get to know each other. (These are your sisters-in-Christ and partners for the journey.)
2. Remind everyone that this is a safe place for sharing hearts and prayer requests. Everything must be kept confidential within the group. Try to stay on topic so everyone has time to share.
3. Introduce yourselves and briefly share a little information—favorite food, hobby, or anything else you think is important, fun, or interesting.
4. Ask everyone to describe their current prayer life and the ways they'd like to improve it?
5. Watch the *Introduction* video and close your time together in prayer. Prepare to dive into *Week One* of your workbook.

Week One—Pray this Way

1. Open in prayer. Share your overall impressions and greatest takeaways.
2. Watch the summary video for *Week One.*
3. Ask someone to read **Matthew 6:5-13** aloud.
4. Now read *the Lord's Prayer* aloud together (**Matthew 6:9-13**).
5. Ask everyone to share how their understanding of the Lord's Prayer has been enhanced, changed, or grown through the study.
6. How does Jesus' prayer life encourage you to pray? Discuss verses and questions 1-6 from *Day One, Like Jesus.*
7. Which prompt from Jesus' prayer are you looking forward to diving deeper into? Explain.
8. Close your time together in prayer and ask God to prepare your hearts for the upcoming days together.

Week Two—Worship

1. Open in prayer. Share overall impressions of the lesson.
2. Watch the summary video for *Week Two*.
3. Read **the Lord's Prayer** aloud together (**Matthew 6:9-13**).
4. Which aspect of God's character did you find easiest to worship? Which one meant the most to you? Why?
5. Which verses encouraged your heart?
6. How does worshipping God change the direction of your prayers and alter your perspective?
7. **Revelation 4:1-11** records the apostle John's description of Heaven and the honor that's ascribed to the Lord. Read these verses aloud and then discuss how they impact your view of God.
8. Close your time together in prayer—begin and close with *worship*.

Week Three—Submission

1. Open in prayer. Share your greatest takeaway and favorite verses.
2. Watch the corresponding video for *Week Three*.
3. Submission is not easy; it requires an enormous amount of trust. Which day of the week helped make surrender a little easier for you?
4. Ask a volunteer to read **Matthew 5:3-6** aloud—discuss questions 1 and 2 from *Day One, God's Authority*.
5. Discuss questions 1 and 2 from *Day Four, Seeking God's Will*.
6. Share answers to question 2 from *Day Six, Immediate Obedience*.
7. How does fixing your eyes on Jesus inspire you to follow Him?
8. Close your time together in prayer—focus on *submission*.

Week Four—Thanksgiving

1. Open in prayer. Share about your most inspiring day of the week.
2. Watch the corresponding video for *Week Four*.
3. How is your prayer life improving? What areas are you struggling with?
4. How has counting your blessings and thanking God impacted your attitude?
5. *Day One, Entering In*—have someone read **Psalm 100:1-5** aloud, then discuss question 2.
6. *Day Two, Lavish Benefits*—read **Psalm 103:1-22**; discuss questions 1-2.
7. *Day Three, Every Blessing*—read **Ephesians 1:3-14**; discuss questions 1-2.
8. Conclude your time together in prayer—focus on *thanksgiving*.

Week Five—Requests

1. Open in prayer. Share your biggest takeaway from the week.
2. Watch the corresponding video for *Week Five*.
3. Share how worshipping God and thanking Him for past provisions helps you to trust Him with your current daily needs.
4. Which aspect of prayer do you need to work on—assuredly, persistently, earnestly, specifically, boldly, expectantly, or faithfully? Explain.
5. *Day One, Assuredly*—read **Psalm 71:5-8** and discuss question 2.
6. *Day Five—Boldly*—read **Mark 5:21-34** and discuss questions 1 and 2.
7. *Day Six, Expectantly*—discuss Elijah's expectant prayers and answer questions 1 and 2.
8. Close your time together by praying for your specific *requests*.

Week Six—Confession

1. Open in prayer. Share your thoughts on the lesson.
2. Watch the corresponding video for *Week Six*.
3. Share about when you first confessed Jesus as Lord and Savior.
4. *Day Three, Removing Barriers*—take turns reading **Psalm 51:1-19**, and answer questions 1 and 2.
5. *Day Four, Dead to Sin*—read **2 Corinthians 5:17**; discuss question 2.
6. *Day Five, Forgiving Like God*—share your answers for questions 1 and 2.
7. *Day Six, Repentance and Revival*—read **2 Chronicles 7:14** and then turn to **Psalm 85:1-13** and discuss questions 1 and 2.
8. Conclude your time together in prayer—praise God aloud, pray for each other's needs, and then take a moment for silent *confession*.

Week Seven—Protection

1. Open in prayer. Share your takeaway from the week.
2. Watch the corresponding video for *Week Seven*.
3. *Day One, Draw Near*—read **James 4:7-8**; discuss questions 1 and 2.
4. *Day Two, Overcoming Worry*—read **1 Peter 5:7** and **Matthew 6:25-34**; discuss questions 1 and 2.
5. *Day Three, To Strengthen*—read **2 Peter 1:3**, discuss questions 1 and 2.
6. *Day Four, Armor of God*—read **Ephesians 6:10-18**; discuss all the pieces of armor and how they help you stand firm.
7. *Day Seven, Salvation and Spirit*—discuss questions 1 and 2.
8. Close in prayer—worship, give thanks, share needs, ask for *protection*.

Week Eight—Prayer Prompts

1. Open in prayer. Share overall impressions from the week—greatest takeaway and encouragement.
2. Watch the corresponding video for *Week Eight*.
3. Ask everyone to read their favorite verses from pages 130-131.
4. Share how your prayer life is growing as a result of practicing it every day.
5. Share testimonies of how God is answering prayers.
6. Share needs that you are still waiting for answers on
7. Which *Prayer Prompt* inspired your prayers most?
8. Close your time by praying with and for each other. If you're comfortable, share one of your prayers from the week with the group.

Week Nine—Prayer Devotions

1. Open in prayer. Share impressions from the week and the entire study.
2. Watch the corresponding video for *Week Nine*.
3. Ask for a few volunteers to read **Psalm 104:1-35**.
4. How has reading your Bible helped inspire and deepen your prayer life?
5. How does praising God first, affect the flow of your prayers?
6. How does thanking the Lord shift your perspective?
7. How is confession keeping the lines of communication open with God?
8. Read **Genesis 16:13** *(It's written at the top of Day Four, Our Comfort.)*
9. Conclude your time together in prayer. Give each other hugs and continue to keep in touch and pray for each other.

So Grateful

For my Dad, who has been an extension of my Heavenly Father's love for me. Dad, you are loving, kind, strong, and caring. You are a man of character and honor. I thank you for loving me every moment of my life; for welcoming me into this world and into your heart. Thank you for trips to the park, pushes on the swing, for trips to Disneyland, and fun times visiting your work. Thank you for bubble gum ice cream cones and root beer floats. Thank you, Dad, for always being there for me—in times of celebration and through difficult occasions. Thank you for being you.

Thank you for designing the heart that is found throughout this book and for bringing the pieces of the cover together. I love you!

A Bit About Tracy

First and foremost, I am a woman who loves the Lord with all her heart; I can't imagine doing life without Him. I am married to a wonderful man, and I'm a mother of two grown men (who used to be little boys). I am a daughter, a sister, a friend, a neighbor. I spend much of my time writing Bible studies, devotionals, freelance articles, and my weekly blog. I write to inspire others to deepen their relationships with Jesus through the study of His Word. A great passion of mine is serving in women's ministry and teaching others about the hope, joy, peace, and confidence that is rightfully theirs as a child of God. I enjoy taking walks outside and enjoy traveling and taking pictures (the photos on my book covers are taken by me). Although I find delight in all flowers, roses are my favorite fragrant blooms.

Even if our lives don't look exactly alike, I'm sure we have plenty in common. I'm so happy to have you join me on this journey and hope that you find some encouragement as we walk with the Lord together.

More Ways to Connect

Website: www.beblessedandinspired.com

YouTube Videos:

www.youtube.com/@beblessedandinspiredwithtracy/playlists

Spotify Podcast: Be Blessed and Inspired with Tracy Hill

Blog: tracyhillbeblessed.substack.com

My Books: amazon.com/author/beblessedandinspired

Esty Shop: BeBlessedandInspired - Etsy

Website

Videos

Podcast

Books

Etsy

Blog

Additional Inspiration

Available on Amazon.com

A Daughter of the King: Gaining Confidence as a Child of God (A Bible Study)—God's desire is for you to discover the confidence and rich blessings of your identity which are found in Jesus Christ. You will to learn to fight off the lies of insecurity with Truth. You are meant to live in victory as *A Daughter of the King*. You are royalty.

Colossians: Set Your Heart on Things Above (A Bible Study)—We will experience a glorious shift in our perspective by meditating on the supremacy of Christ and on our fullness in Him. Our relationships will be greatly impacted. The peace, hope, and joy of Christ will help us overcome and persevere.

Matthew: Your Kingdom Come (A Bible Study)—By studying this amazing Gospel, we will come to know Jesus better and, as a result, fall even more deeply in love with Him. We will hear His teachings, witness His miracles, see His power, and feel His love. Encountering Jesus changes our lives forever.

Worship and Wonder: Faith-Filled Devotions—Throughout this devotional, you and I will meditate on God's Word and find comfort in His lavish love. We will be overcome with wonder and worship His holy Name. Every page is meant to remind us of our blessings, fill us with hope, and grow our faith.

Promise and Possibilities: Hope-Filled Devotions—You will glimpse the promise that life holds and the possibility of all that can be when you place your hope in Jesus. He is truly the One who holds the key.

Confidence and Crowns: Devotions for A Daughter of the King—The devotions, stories, and Scripture you will encounter, are all intended to point you to the reality of who you are in God's eyes. It is time to put aside your doubts and insecurities and live a life of confidence.

Lilies and Lemonade: Joy-Filled Devotions—*Lilies and Lemonade* represents two philosophies which hold the key to optimistic living. A joy-filled perspective is available to us when we look at life with the proper Jesus-filled mindset.

www.ingramcontent.com/pod-product-compliance
Lightning Source LLC
Chambersburg PA
CBHW050454110426
42743CB00017B/3359